IN PURSUIT OF PRESTIGE

IN PURSUIT OF PRESTIGE

Strategy and Competition in U.S. Higher Education

Dominic J. Brewer, Susan M. Gates, and Charles A. Goldman

Transaction Publishers

New Brunswick (U.S.A.) and London (U.K.)

Library of Congress Catalog Number: 2001037347
ISBN: 0-7658-0056-X
Printed in the United States of America

Library of Congress Cataloging-in-Publication Data

Brewer, Dominic J.
    In pursuit of prestige : strategy and competition in U.S. higher education /
Dominic J. Brewer, Susan M. Gates and Charles A. Goldman.
        p. cm.
    Includes bibliographical references and index.
    ISBN 0-7658-0056-X (alk. paper)
    1. Education, Higher—Economic aspects—United States. 2. Education, Higher—Social aspects—United States. 3. Prestige. 4. Educational surveys—United States. I. Gates, Susan M., 1968- II. Goldman, Charles A., 1964- III. Title.

LC67 .62 .B75 2001
378.73—dc21   2001037347

Contents

List of Tables

List of Figures

Preface

Higher education is widely regarded as an American success story. The sector educates unprecedented numbers of students and produces an unrivaled research base. By almost any measure, it is a vital part of the U.S. economy and society. Yet, there is concern that the sector is ill-equipped to adapt to the changing environment in which it finds itself. The information revolution, an aging population, and a declining fiscal base all present major challenges to the nation's colleges and universities. Higher education's performance is being seriously challenged by those who believe that institutions are inefficient or self-serving.

In this book we describe the results of a two-year study of higher education in the United States designed to shed some light on these issues. Unlike previous researchers on the sector, we examine higher education from an *industry* perspective and focus specifically on the conduct of the industry's providers. In so doing, we examine how institutions serve customers in four identifiable markets that generate revenues (student enrollment, research funding, public fiscal support, and private giving). We describe and analyze institutions' investment, pricing and marketing behaviors, and the nature of competition among schools.

The research underlying the analyses was generously supported by the Alfred P. Sloan Foundation, with additional support from TIAA-CREF.

This research is based on information gathered in 1996 through a series of twenty-six site visits to diverse types of colleges and universities throughout the United States. We are indebted to the presidents, vice presidents, deans, faculty, staff, and students of these institutions. To arrange the site visits, we contacted the presidents of the institutions and requested their cooperation. As a condition of participation, we promised them that we would keep confidential the identities of their institutions and the individuals we interviewed. Therefore, we cannot recognize them by name, but we thank them for their willingness to participate in this study, their candor, the organizational effort involved in coordinating our visits, and their comments on an early version of the manuscript.

We also appreciate the insights and comments of others who reviewed previous manuscript versions: Jesse Ausubel, James Dewar, Irwin Feller, Marie Gates, Roger Geiger, Steve Goldman, Patti Gumport, Brett Hammond, as well as seminar participants at RAND, Lehigh University, the White House Office of Science and Technology Policy, and the Triple Helix II Conference. Several publishers and their anonymous reviewers also provided helpful criticism.

We would like to thank Marc Chun, Tessa Kaganoff, and Ann Stone for their assistance conducting the site visits and for their efforts during other aspects of this research endeavor. In addition, we thank the following individuals for their participation at various stages of this project: Beth Benjamin, Roger Benjamin, Stephen Carroll, Maryann Gray, Robert Lempert, William Lewis, William Massy, George Park, Matthew Sanders, Darius Sankey, Cathy Stasz, Daochi Tong, and Laura Zakaras. Judy Lewis and Judy Rolhoff were instrumental in placing this book with its publisher.

We want to place these ideas before a wide audience and have therefore written this book with minimal technical detail. But some questions are suitable for treatment with more sophisticated methods from economics, statistics, and organizational behavior. During this project, we prepared a collection of technical papers to provide greater depth, particularly in quantitative detail, to support the analyses in this book. The collection of technical papers is entitled *In Pursuit of Prestige: Strategy and Competition in U.S. Higher Education, Technical Papers* (Brewer, Gates, and Goldman 2001). It is available through RAND at no charge under document number DRU-2541. To order this publication from RAND, contact Distribution Services at (310) 451-7002; Fax (310) 451-6915; Internet: order @rand.org.

The ideas in this book resulted from objective reflection on detailed and revealing information from the participants in the twenty-six site visits. We supplemented the site visits with analysis of available statistics about this industry at the institutional and national levels. The site visits provided us with rich organizational detail and many ideas both conventional and provocative. The sites, however, represent only a small proportion of the total number of institutions in the United States. This study is therefore exploratory. It is a first step, not the last word. As the researchers and authors, we believe that the themes we develop here should be subject to much further analysis to support or refute the power of our framework. We welcome that scrutiny and gladly accept responsibility for the work presented here.

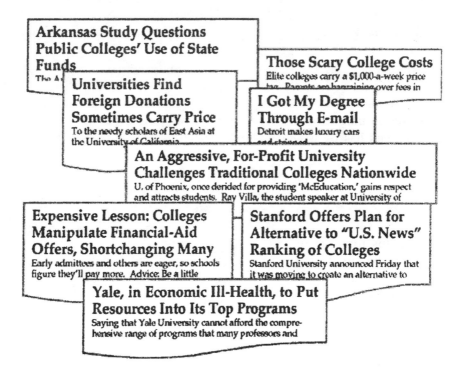

Arkansas Study Questions Public Colleges' Use of State Funds
The A

Those Scary College Costs
Elite colleges carry a $1,000-a-week price tag. Parents are bargaining over fees in

Universities Find Foreign Donations Sometimes Carry Price
To the needy scholars of East Asia at the University of California

I Got My Degree Through E-mail
Detroit makes luxury cars and shipped

An Aggressive, For-Profit University Challenges Traditional Colleges Nationwide
U. of Phoenix, once derided for providing 'McEducation,' gains respect and attracts students. Ray Villa, the student speaker at University of

Expensive Lesson: Colleges Manipulate Financial-Aid Offers, Shortchanging Many
Early admittees and others are eager, so schools figure they'll pay more. Advice: Be a little

Stanford Offers Plan for Alternative to "U.S. News" Ranking of Colleges
Stanford University announced Friday that it was moving to create an alternative to

Yale, in Economic Ill-Health, to Put Resources Into Its Top Programs
Saying that Yale University cannot afford the comprehensive range of programs that many professors and

1

Introduction:
A New Perspective on U.S. Higher Education

Higher education is widely regarded as an American success story. Over 3,000 colleges and universities across the nation educate 15 million students of all backgrounds in a vast array of programs and sustain an unrivaled research base. Growth over the past one hundred years has been phenomenal, prompting education leader Clark Kerr to recently describe it as a "golden century" for higher education (Kerr, 1997). By almost any measure, higher education is a vital part of the U.S. economy and society, critical to our national well-being: it educates our citizens; produces both basic and applied research; supports national security; generates spin-off technology; and helps improve quality of life in communities throughout the country by supporting cultural, recreational, and continuing education activities. Much of this success is due to the tremendous innovations that have occurred over the past two centuries.

Yet news stories about higher education paint a much more negative picture. Recent headlines, opposite, provide just a few examples.[1] Colleges and universities are in cut-throat competition for students and financial resources. Long-established colleges face challenges from more customer-oriented, for-profit institutions. This competition is driving down the quality of higher education. These headlines also suggest that higher education has missed the boat in one respect or another. Why are schools spending tremendous resources on athletic teams when sports are clearly not intrinsic to the primary mission of a college or university? In the midst of the information revolution, traditional institutions of higher education are struggling to incorporate new technology into the education process. Many constituencies, particularly state governments and students, are

1

troubled by rising costs. In spite of increased customer interest, institutions are resisting the emergence of sources that provide comparative data and rankings to help students make choices.

In response to concerns and changes, some institutions are reallocating their resources and re-examining their approach to providing higher education. Other institutions traditionally seen as passive are making aggressive moves to expand their customer base. However, there is concern that the higher education establishment is ill-equipped to respond to the environment in which it finds itself today. In particular, a rapidly changing economy, demographic shifts, and competition from new providers all present major challenges to the nation's colleges and universities. The sector has come under recent attack for not responding adequately to these trends. Consistent cost increases, the potential inability of several public systems to provide higher education to all citizens who would benefit from it, and a decline in the "quality" of higher education as evinced by measures of student achievement are all cited as evidence of this inadequacy. Moreover, higher education's performance is being seriously questioned by those who believe that the sector is inefficient or self-serving.

What are we to make of these conflicting views of America's higher education industry? On the one hand, it is envied around the world for its success; on the other hand, it is seriously stressed. What framework can we use to understand this conflicted higher education industry? This book attempts to answer those questions.

Traditional research on higher education typically focuses upon specific aspects of the sector but does not attempt to understand the higher education sector *overall* or how the parts are related. For example, much of the previous literature focuses on specific types of institutions (e.g., research universities, community colleges), constituent groups (e.g., students, faculty), or a single issue (e.g., tuition and cost increases, governance or administrative concerns, student financial aid, minority participation). This is hardly surprising, given the complexity and size of higher education. It does mean, however, that while we may be able to learn something about each of these topics from previous studies, we would unlikely be able to draw linkages among them or put them in a broader context.

The purpose of this book is to shed some light on the issues raised by the headlines and claims discussed above by explicitly examining the higher education sector as a whole. Our approach is comprehensive and is guided by the industry study perspective. Within the general industry study framework, we focus our attention on the conduct, especially the strategic choices and competitive behavior, of providers in the higher education industry. The examination of conduct is organized around four key markets that generate revenues (student enrollments, research funding, public fiscal support, and private giving) for institutions. This analysis is based on the results of a two-year study of higher education in the United States, drawing on site visits to twenty-six diverse institutions across the country. We describe the conduct of these institutions, that is, the strategies they pursue and the nature of competition among schools. The focus on strategy and competition allows us to understand institutional behavior and to address the issue of financial health. It also permits some well-grounded conjectures about industry performance—the successes and failures of the sector and its prospects for the future.

An examination of strategy and competition brings out the ways in which higher education is like other industries. Thinking about higher education as an industry will strike some readers immediately as rather strange, perhaps even preposterous for a variety of reasons. For example, most universities and colleges do not seek to make profits for shareholders but instead try to satisfy the needs of multiple constituencies: they provide a complex set of educational, psychological, and social experiences to students; government—at all levels—is a major player; and often intangible social benefits accrue from their activities. While we do not dispute these points, we hope to show that, in fact, higher education is in many ways like traditional industries. It has several sets of "customers": students, alumni, employers, corporations, governments, and private individuals. These customers provide revenues to different enterprises through four distinct revenue markets: student enrollments, research funding, public fiscal support, and private giving. The enterprises compete and cooperate with each other in these four revenue markets, and different customers provide revenue through different markets. Institutional behavior is both determined and constrained by what is happening in these markets. We believe that the industry study framework generates useful insights about institutional behaviors and the overall performance of the sector. We ask skeptical readers to judge the approach by whether this is indeed the case.

Studying Strategic Behavior in Higher Education

This book provides a description and analysis of the conduct of providers in the higher education industry and thereby falls within the industry study framework. *Industry study* is a generic term used to describe a variety of research approaches in which the unit of analysis is the set of economic entities serving an identifiable market. Figure 1.1 provides a comprehensive illustration of the overarching industry study framework, the *structure-conduct-performance paradigm.*[2] According to the paradigm, an industry is governed by some basic supply and conditions: what is the customer base, what do customers want, how much are they willing to pay; what can providers produce and at what cost, and what are the different production technologies available to producers. The answers to these questions determine the basic market conditions influencing the structure of the market. Market structure is defined by several factors, including the number of buyers and sellers, the similarity or difference in the nature of goods or services sold, and the existence of entry barriers, such as up-front costs that must be paid before one can participate in the market. Market structure in turn influences the conduct of providers in the industry. Conduct includes the decisions firms make and the behavior that follows from those decisions. It encompasses investment decisions, pricing strategies, marketing strategies, and so forth. Industry performance is related to what the industry actually does and how that influences customers, producers, and society as a whole—how well the industry accomplishes what it is supposed to do. The industry study framework posits that industry performance is determined by the conduct of firms under the influence of market structure, the basic supply and demand conditions in a particular market, as well as public policy related to the industry.

The ultimate goal of a typical industry study is to provide some assessment of the performance of the industry. An industry's performance can be evaluated from many different perspectives: the customer, the shareholders of the firm, the workers of the firm, the government, etc. The benefit that these different parties derive from the industry depends not only on the total value of output produced by the firms in the industry but also on the way in which that value is distributed.[3] In order to address the issue of industry performance, it is thus insufficient to measure industry profits. It is also necessary to ask questions such as: who benefits from the activities of this industry; how do they benefit; and how is that benefit distributed among the firms, customers, and society as a whole? Quantifying the answers to these questions and aggregating them into a single measure of industry performance is problematic. The industry study paradigm provides us with a second-best alternative by pointing out the major performance-related concerns and directing us toward an understanding of what factors influence performance.

A comprehensive understanding of every aspect of an industry and how it affects performance is impossible to achieve. Normally, an industry study (or a study that falls within the industry study framework) tackles a more modest goal—examining a single relationship (e.g.; the relationship between market structure and conduct) a single issue relevant to the industry (e.g.; the role of entry barriers), or focusing on some subset of firms in the industry. Such industry studies are pieces of a mosaic; as more pieces are included, the overall picture of the industry is elucidated.

Regardless of the specific approach used in an industry study, the first task is to limit the scope by defining the industry one wishes to study. The industrial organization literature suggests that industry (or market) definition is more an art than a science, with no hard and fast rules available to aid the process of definition. A single industry may exhibit a great deal of market segmentation, in which firms identify subpopulations of customers with similar characteristics and focus on meeting their needs, resulting in a situation where different firms are doing very different things. Such segmentation may be a focus of a broadly defined industry study, or it can determine industry boundaries. For example, a study of the restaurant industry might include all establishments that serve prepared food and provide an environment in which that food can be consumed and then consider the development of particular market segments, such as fast-food, fine dining, family-style restaurants. Alternatively, it could focus on fast-food restaurants alone and examine the behavior of institutions in that market segment.

Once the industry has been defined, the basic supply and demand conditions of the industry are described sufficiently to set the context for the analysis. This includes pinpointing the objective that firms in the industry are pursuing. In most industry settings, it is relatively easy to identify objectives: firms strive to maximize profit.

Figure 1.1
Industry Study Framework

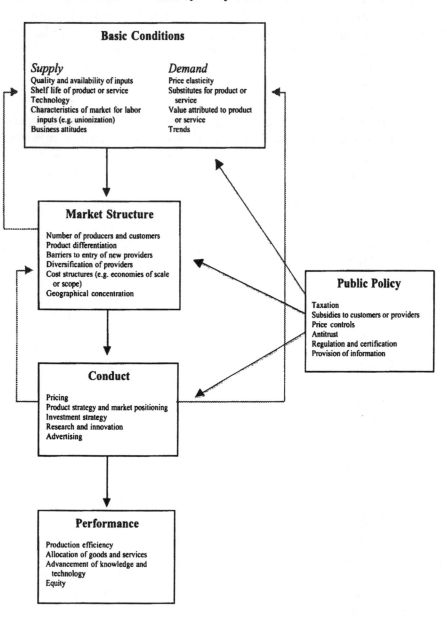

Source: Adapted from Scherer and Ross (1990).

However, even if firms are assumed to be profit maximizing, the nature of the production process, the goods or services produced, the competitive structure of the industry, and information asymmetry between the buyer and seller can influence industry behavior and the overall profitability of the industry. In classic for-profit industries it is appropriate, even useful, to focus on one product market and analyze that particular market because overlap among markets is small and organizational cross-subsidies are zero or minimal. In higher education, to understand the operation of any one market one needs a simultaneous understanding of all of the key revenue markets because of overlapping production processes and cross-subsidies in many institutions. This point also applies to regulated industries such as energy and telecommunications where cross-subsidies between regulated and unregulated business lines may be important.

Although industry study methods have not been frequently applied to higher education, there appears to be increasing interest in these methods. For example, Roger Noll (1998) recently edited a book that applies a market-based analysis (similar to our four revenue markets presented in Chapter 3) to study research universities. Feller (1996) examined competition among research universities. Zemsky, Shaman, and Iannozzi (1997) are developing techniques to analyze how institutions operate in the market for students. Others have applied game theoretic methods to examine the strategic behavior among colleges and universities in specific markets, such as financial aid, or to examine management issues in higher education (Carmichael 1988, Masten 1995, and Toma 1986).

Although based on description, the goal of an industry analysis is to generalize beyond available descriptive information. In developing such generalizations, there is always a tradeoff between making precise statements about a small set of institutions or behaviors, and making less precise statements about a larger set of institutions and behaviors. Most analyses of higher education employ the first option, precisely analyzing a narrow set of behaviors or types of institutions. Our approach is distinctive because it is more comprehensive, covering the full spectrum of higher education institutions and activities. It is an ambitious undertaking, and we do not purport to have a complete understanding of strategy and competition in higher education. However, we do believe that this book provides a useful and significant first step in that direction. In addition, we rely on new qualitative data that provide a descriptive foundation upon which we base the development of a conceptual framework describing position, strategy, and competition in higher education.

New Qualitative Data

In order to learn about the strategies pursued by institutions of higher education, we conducted a series of site visits at a wide variety of colleges and universities around the nation. During each trip, we met with the president and other administrators of the institution, faculty, and students. We solicited their opinions regarding the goals of the institution, plans for achieving those goals, and general perceptions of market conditions. We were particularly interested in understanding the most pressing issues facing each institution, the institution's role in the higher education system, and strategies for filling that role. We also took time to observe campus life (the interactions of students, for example), physical surroundings (buildings, landscaping), and classroom activities. (More details on the site visit methodology may be found in the appendix.)

In all, the study team conducted interviews at 26 institutions and met with approximately 200 administrators, students, and faculty. We visited colleges and universities in all geographic regions of the country—the Northeast, the Midwest, the South, and the West. Some were elite research universities. Some were liberal arts colleges. Others were comprehensive public institutions. Some were community colleges. Others were for-profit (proprietary) schools. Our sample included schools that were large and small; urban, suburban and rural; rich and poor; secular and religious. In other words, we tried to capture as far as was practicable (given time and monetary constraints) some of the incredible diversity that exists in U.S. higher education at the institutional level.

Our observations form the basis of the analyses presented in this book. Our analysis is therefore observation driven. We did *not* formulate hypotheses and then attempt to "test" these in the field to validate any theory or model. In order to ensure candid responses we promised all participants complete confidentiality. We are, of course, subject to the limitations of this method of research. In many cases, we must rely on the statements of individual interviewees, especially where we cannot confirm these statements by reference to other interviews or documentary evidence. We are confident that the pictures of the institutions we present are substantially accurate, especially in the key dimensions of position and strategy we discuss. As part of our effort, we sent a draft of this book to the presidents of 26 institutions we visited, soliciting their comments. Their comments reflect support and approval for the framework we developed. In addition, we specifically told the presidents of the six institutions treated in depth in Chapter 5 which section was about their institutions and asked for their feedback. In five of the six cases, the presidents took no issue with our often stark portraits. In one case, the president provided an alternate characterization of a certain specific strategic choice and we revised the narrative to allow the possibility of either that view or our original view.

Throughout this volume, we cite examples of what we were told or what we have inferred from what we were told, but in no case do we provide information that would permit the identification of any school or individual within it. We promised that confidentiality as a condition of our interviews and we believe that we would never have had the candid discussions of sometimes painful circumstances without those promises. We supplement the site visit data with information and insights gained from secondary sources, including newspapers and academic research, and through an examination of quantitative data available from the U.S. Department of Education, the National Science Foundation, the Council on Aid to Education, and other organizations.

Any study of higher education owes a great debt to the careful collection of statistics by these organizations. This book includes a few basic statistics to describe and define the higher education industry. For those readers desiring to find additional details underlying the statistics we present or to explore other aspects of the industry, an excellent place to start is at the World Wide Web site maintained by the National Center for Education Statistics at the U.S. Department of Education. As of t this writing, that web site is located at www.nces.ed.gov. The web site contains many statistical publications on education in web-readable and downloadable formats. Another fine resource is the National Science Foundation's CASPAR on the web, located at www.caspar.nsf.gov.

Overview of the Book

Our observations of higher education institutions and conversations with their leaders revealed a fascinating picture of the changing environment facing the sector and the conduct of institutions of higher education—both how they respond to changes in the basic market conditions and how they interact with their competitors.

While the industry study paradigm includes basic conditions, market structure, conduct, public policy, and performance, the central focus of this book is the conduct (or strategic behavior) of institutions of higher education. As a result we naturally consider certain elements of basic conditions, market structure, and public policy that define the context in which institutions act strategically. In particular, we conclude that both an institution's present *position* as well as its *strategy* affect its ability to compete for scarce resources in the four key revenue markets of student enrollments, research funding, public fiscal support, and private giving. Institutional position is measured in terms of the stock of two assets we later define: reputation and prestige. Strategy entails decisions about which markets to participate in, how broadly and deeply to participate in each market and whether to attempt to build prestige and/or reputation. This view of institutional strategy combines an analysis of industry-level patterns with a bottom-up perspective of behavior in the industry.

The remainder of the book elaborates on these themes. We begin Chapter 2 by describing the context of higher education. We define the boundaries of the higher education industry and provide a brief overview of the industry's basic conditions and the key revenue markets in which providers compete for resources. We then turn to the heart of the book, an analysis of site visit data emphasizing the strategic behavior of institutions.

Chapter 3 offers an overarching framework for strategic decisions and classifies both the position of institutions and the strategies we observed. Chapter 4 describes in more detail the manifestation of these positions and strategies in each institutional revenue market. We describe the characteristics of the market and relate those characteristics to institutional position and strategy. We then try to explain what strategies are possible in the market and how strategic behavior affects customers and other institutions in the industry.

Chapter 5 relates overall institutional strategies to the current positions and investment patterns that are required to support those strategies. We define institutional financial health in two ways: enough revenues to cover operating costs and a strategy consistent with investment. We illustrate the relationships between resource allocation—including investments in reputation and prestige—and financial health by focusing on six institutions that we visited. The chapter concludes by drawing together the insights gained from these case studies. We generalize the insights to a broader spectrum of institutions, using quantitative data sources.

Chapter 6 summarizes our main results and reviews the usefulness of the industry study framework, including the limitations of this research. Based on the main results, we draw out the implications of position, strategy, and competition for the various customers of the U.S. higher education industry.

Notes

1. The news stories are cited in the references: Dodd (1997), Gose (1999), Gubernick and Ebeling, (1997), Kotch (1997), Lords (1999), Ray (1997), Selingo (1999), Strosnider (1997), Suggs (1999b), and Weiss (1997).
2. This framework is described in Scherer and Ross (1990) and is attributed to Edward Mason.
3. *Value added* is a term used to describe the difference between the value that stakeholders place on the outputs of the industry and the value they place on the inputs.

2

Basic Conditions and Market Structure
of the Higher Education Industry

In order to make sense of the conduct of firms in an industry, it is first necessary to understand the context in which the behavior is occurring. This includes the basic supply and demand features, the structure of the market, and the objectives of institutions. Developing such an understanding is not a straightforward task because of the size and complexity of the higher education industry, the multiple constituents that impose conflicting demands on institutions, and the number of significant social considerations. Further complicating analysis is the fact that many institutions do not have a clearly articulated economic goal such as profit maximization.[1] In this chapter we define and lay out some of the basic features of the U.S. higher education industry, setting the context for an analysis of strategic behavior in the industry. In so doing, we pay particular attention to the four key revenue markets in which institutions operate: student enrollments, research funding, public fiscal support, and private giving. We conclude the chapter by defining the objectives of institutions and describing some key features of the industry structure.

Defining the Higher Education Industry

In our analysis, the higher education industry is defined as *the set of enterprises that award two-year, four-year, and/or graduate degrees*. The production of degrees is thus a litmus test for inclusion in our analysis. In adopting this definition, we recognize that higher education enterprises engage in many other activities—they conduct research, award professional certificates, and perform community service. However, an entity that does any or all of these things without offering degrees is not part of the higher education industry as we have defined it. In particular, we exclude institutions that offer only certificates in vocational areas but no degrees and institutions that perform research activities but offer no degrees. This definition implies that enterprises in the higher education industry might compete with firms outside of the industry in one of the key markets. For example, research universities compete with government labs, private nonprofit organizations, and private industry for research dollars. Many institutions of higher education compete with nondegree granting institutions, private sector employers, and the military for students' time.

In 1995 there were 9,962 institutions providing post-secondary education, that is, schooling beyond K-12 (*Digest of Education Statistics*, 1997). Of this number, 3,706 were identified as "institutions of higher education"—which grant at least associate's or bachelor's degrees. Most of these institutions are known as "colleges" or "universities." The remaining 6,256 were identified as "vocational institutions." These institutions may grant certificates but do not award degrees. Figure 2.1 depicts the relationship of the higher education industry as we have defined it to the broader postsecondary education sector.

Four Key Revenue Markets

Higher education institutions operate in a variety of different markets, sell a range of products, and serve multiple customers. In this

Figure 2.1
Defining the U.S. Higher Education Industry

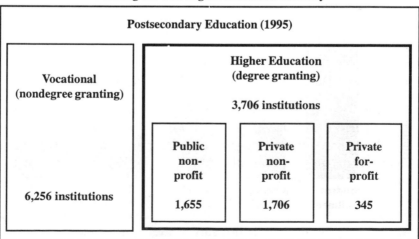

text, we focus on the four major environs in which schools operate and compete with one another. Since each corresponds to a source of revenue for an institution, we shall call them *revenue markets*: student enrollments, research funding, public fiscal support, and private giving.[2] Any given school may operate only in the market for students; others may compete in all four. In addition to the four key revenue markets, we mention other revenue markets only briefly here.

Chapter 4 focuses on the strategic choices and interactions of institutions in each of the four key revenue markets. The volume of technical papers described in the preface (Brewer, Gates, and Goldman 2000) addresses, in some depth, background features of the major revenue markets. The companion volume discusses demand characteristics, market segmentation, price setting, market signals, and outcomes in each market. The background material also contains additional quantitative material related to each market.

As mentioned below, the revenue markets are not of equal importance either for individual institutions or for the industry as a whole. To gauge the rough prominence of each market for the industry as a whole, we have provided recent figures on the overall revenues in each market in Figure 2.2.

Figure 2.2
Total Revenues in the U.S. Higher Education Industry, 1993–94

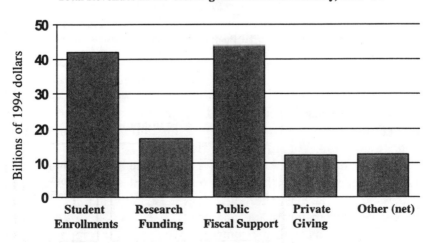

Revenue Market

Student Enrollments

Student enrollment is the lifeblood of the overwhelming majority of higher education institutions. Students are the reason for their very existence. In 1994, student enrollments generated $42 billion, not including the revenues recognized as public fiscal support. Revenues from student enrollments are second only to public fiscal support, and only by a slight margin.

An industry perspective focuses attention on institutional positioning in the student enrollment market and the manner in which schools attract students. This viewpoint highlights several interesting and important aspects of the current state of the higher education industry—whether schools compete on the basis of price or quality or both, the type of products offered, and the extent to which some institutions are buffered from the vagaries of the marketplace.

Research Funding

Many higher education institutions conduct basic and applied research. In total, research sponsors provided $17 billion in 1994 to higher education. This total makes research funding the third largest market overall. Institutions perform research for a diverse customer base that includes federal, state, and local governments; philanthropic organizations; and private profit-making concerns. Federal government research funding is dominant, but state governments, foundations, and, increasingly, industry and other organizations also buy research services. Colleges and universities compete with other providers—private research companies (for-profit and nonprofit) and public research laboratories—for this type of revenue.

Public Fiscal Support

Government (particularly the federal government) provides a substantial amount of research funding to institutions of higher education. In addition, government (particularly state government) provides fiscal support to institutions for other purposes. In 1994, higher education received $44 billion in public fiscal support.[3] This total makes public fiscal support the largest revenue market. Because governments are significant customers, it is crucial to understand their relationships with the industry. Much of this support is provided to specific institutions through political and bureaucratic (nonmarket) processes. We analyze these mechanisms of direct support and the associated government relations with higher education.

Private Giving

Institutions seek to raise funds from a variety of private givers—foundations, alumni, corporations, and other individuals. The private sector, through both organizations and individuals, provides financial resources to the higher education industry in several ways, such as altruistic cash donations, targeted gifts, or purchases of specific goods and services. Once again, an industry study requires an understanding of how institutions operate in the market for private giving and the strategies they pursue to maximize revenue-generating capabilities in this market. Although the private giving total in 1994 was the smallest of the four revenue markets at $12 billion, these funds allow some institutions crucial flexibility in their operations.

Other Revenue Markets

Institutions receive revenues from other sources as well. The major components of these revenues are sales and services, hospitals, auxiliary enterprises, and independent operations. Sales and services include revenue from activities that provide goods or services to individuals outside of the institution. Such activities include publishing, film production, and agricultural produce. Auxiliary enterprises are business operations that furnish services to the students, faculty, or staff, such as housing, food service, student health services, parking, telecommunications, and intercollegiate athletics. Independent operations generally refer to specific research laboratories operated for the federal government. Some institutions have even more idiosyncratic sources of revenue, such as trademarks and patent royalties, fees from shopping malls, and land leased to outside organizations for many different purposes.

Since our focus is on the education and research mission of higher education, rather than its operation of these ancillary enterprises, we show the net revenue from other sources, after subtracting the costs of operating hospitals, auxiliary enterprises, and independent operations.[4] This net revenue was about $12 billion in 1994 (out of a gross of $51 billion). Although the revenue generated outside the four key revenue markets is substantial, it is not materially larger than any of the individual four key revenue markets. The heterogeneity and idiosyncratic nature of these revenue sources make it difficult to examine them in a systematic way.

Institutional Objectives

What objectives do higher education institutions pursue? What drives the conduct of institutions in each of these revenue markets? As mentioned above, industry studies commonly assume that firms are motivated by a desire to maximize profit. As a general description, the for-profit firm serves the interests of its owners or shareholders. That is, the firms pursue activities that yield the greatest financial return. In the higher education industry today, almost all institutions are nonprofit organizations. This complicates our analysis in two respects.

First, it forces us to consider the objectives of nonprofit organizations and how those objectives contrast with the objectives of for-profit organizations. Second, it implies that we must consider the interactions among firms with very different objectives. An industry perspective suggests that these differences in objectives might have significant implications for market conduct and ultimately industry performance.

Approximately half of all postsecondary schools are for-profit (proprietary), but most of these are nondegree granting institutions and hence do not fall within our higher education industry definition. However, degree granting for-profit institutions do exist and are beginning to receive a lot of attention in the popular press if not in the academic literature. For example, the University of Phoenix, a for-profit institution that serves working adults, currently enrolls over 75,000 students at 92 sites in 17 states, provinces, and territories. Measured on the basis of enrollment, it has become one of the largest institutions in the country, public or private, nonprofit or for-profit. Enrollment has increased over 100 percent in four years (see Gubernick and Ebeling 1997, and Schmidt 1997; up-to-date information is available at www.phoenix.edu).

Prior studies of higher education have all but ignored the for-profit sector. Part of the reason for this is that standard reports of national education statistics do not distinguish between private, nonprofit institutions and private, for-profit institutions. As a result, it is difficult to examine systematically the markets currently being served by for-profit institutions and, perhaps more important, the markets into which for-profit institutions are expanding. However, from an industry perspective, the distinction between for-profit and nonprofit institutions is at least as important as the distinction between public and private, nonprofit institutions.

Another reason for the lack of attention given to for-profit institutions is the historical dominance of the higher education industry by nonprofit entities likely stems from the roots of these institutions as first religious and later independent or publicly supported entities. An interesting question is why nonprofit entities continue to dominate. Weisbrod (1988) posits that the relative benefits of nonprofit entities in certain industries stem from what economists term "information asymmetries." In markets where customers are well informed and there is competition, for-profit firms will be efficient and effective; moreover, competition drives a fair allocation of the benefit generated by the industry between customers and producers. When customers lack information, profit-oriented sellers take advantage of this. In such markets, nonprofit organizations play an important role because they do not have the incentive to take advantage of the buyers' lack of information.[5] Higher education is an industry in which consumers are often underinformed in the sense that they cannot objectively evaluate the quality of the service before they actually purchase it. Consumers' inability to evaluate quality before making a purchase is a common feature of service industries. However, the problem is particularly severe in the higher education industry because many of the relevant outcomes are not observed until years later. In addition, the "purchase" of higher education requires substantial investment on the part of the student, not only in terms of direct costs such as room and board but also in terms of indirect costs such as foregone wages or the cost of effort involved in learning. In the higher education industry, the providers have an opportunity to take advantage of relative consumer ignorance and such opportunism can be very costly to the student. As a result, this information asymmetry has important implications for the nature of competition in the higher education industry in general. In particular, it implies that reputation and prestige have an important role to play in the industry. We will return to this issue in the next chapter.

We follow standard industry study convention by assuming that profit maximization is the objective of for-profit institutions. However, it cannot be the objective of nonprofit institutions. The nonprofit enterprise cannot maximize profits. Its nonprofit charter prohibits the enterprise from showing a profit. Instead, any potential profits from one activity are used to subsidize other activities. The activities that receive subsidies in any given nonprofit are activities that are valued by key stakeholders. Howard Bowen has stated a simplified description of this process (Bowen 1981): Colleges and universities "will raise all the money they can and spend all the money they raise." Institutions will spend available funds on valued activities rather than let them appear as "profit"—even temporarily.[6]

Spending the Revenue: Basic Operating Costs and Discretionary Resources

Institutions of higher education generate revenue in the form of tuition, grants and contracts, state appropriation, and private giving from the four major revenue markets plus others, as described above. Revenue generated from students, research, public or private funds and is spent in part on the technology, raw materials, and personnel necessary to supply products to customers in these markets. The mix of spending on inputs into the production process obviously varies among institutions: the goods and services provided by the industry can be produced in a multitude of different ways. Nevertheless, we assume there is some basic cost associated with providing these services in the most efficient manner.[7]

We can split input expenditures into two basic categories: basic operating costs and the residual, discretionary resources (i.e., the difference between the institution's total revenues and its basic costs). Although there is a good deal of research on the production process in higher education that focuses on the determinants of basic costs (Getz and Seigfreid 1991; Hopkins 1990), there is relatively little attention paid to discretionary resources. Figure 2.3 illustrates a typical institution receiving revenue from the various markets and allocating revenue to cover basic operating costs and discretionary resources.

Our focus explicitly is on how these discretionary resources are allocated among *investment, savings, and extra consumption.* Chapter 3 focuses more specifically on investment expenditures. Deciding how to split discretionary resources among investment, savings, and extra consumption is a theme we return to in Chapter 5.

One of the major differences between for-profit and nonprofit institutions is the flexibility they have with respect to the use of these discretionary resources. In particular, for-profit enterprises can give discretionary resources to stakeholders in the form of profit. The stakeholders can then use these profits to buy whatever it is that they want to consume. For-profit firms are thus driven to maximize profit, which they can do by increasing marginal revenue (the additional revenue generated by selling one more unit of a good or service) or reducing marginal costs (the additional cost generated by producing one more unit of a good or service). Nonprofit institutions, on the other hand, cannot distribute discretionary revenue to stakeholders in the form of profits. Since profits must not exceed zero, an implication of the goal of revenue maximization is cost *maximization* subject to the balanced budget constraint. Nonprofit institutions are motivated to increase marginal revenue but do not have a clear interest in minimizing marginal costs. What this means is that the institution will always find a way to spend or invest any revenue it receives.

Figure 2.3
An Institution Allocates Revenue from Five Markets to Basic Operating Costs and Discretionary Revenue

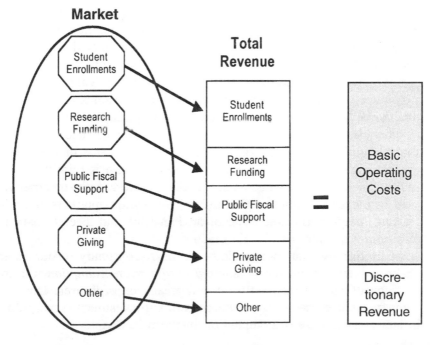

Although some input expenditures provide consumption benefits, from an accounting perspective they appear as costs of operation. For example, an institution of higher education might allocate discretionary resources to the salaries of faculty and staff, amenities for faculty and staff, social and education programs that benefit students, or research infrastructure. To paraphrase the CEO of one for-profit school we visited, the major difference between his institution and nonprofits is that the latter spend their "profits" on fancy furniture whereas his institution's profits are dispersed to shareholders. This difficulty in disentangling basic operating costs from consumption complicates the analysis of higher education as an industry.

Industry Structure, Conduct, and Performance

The behavior of colleges and universities is influenced by their internal objectives. However, an institution does not exist in a vacuum. Institutions interact with both customers and other providers in the four key revenue markets. The results of the decisions of any one institution will be influenced by the activities of other institutions. Our description and analysis of institutional behavior must therefore be examined in the context of the overall structure of the industry within which colleges and universities operate. In addition to explaining institutional conduct within this structure, in Chapter 6 we will use implications of the conduct to shed some light on the performance of the industry as a whole

Market structure is defined by many characteristics, such as the number of buyers and sellers, product differentiation, and barriers to entry. Barriers to entry normally stem from a need to invest resources up front before a firm can successfully operate in the industry and begin to generate revenue. If these investments are not easy to liquidate or convert to another use, they can also pose a barrier to exit. In higher education, these initial investments appear to be significant, particularly among traditional institutions. The sheer cost of building a campus and hiring faculty and staff is substantial. The accreditation system[8] poses additional barriers because institutions generally need the stamp of approval from accreditation boards in order to attract students, yet it takes a great deal of time and investment to achieve accreditation. Barriers to entry and exit such as this influence the nature of competition in the industry.

Product differentiation is an important feature of many industries. What does product differentiation mean in higher education? There are educational products (such as degrees), research products (such as academic journal articles or new patented medicines), and other products (such as sporting events). While some institutions provide all of these, others choose to specialize. However, product differentiation goes well beyond these pedestrian distinctions and can encompass a number of different features of these basic products as well. For example, an institution might focus on providing educational services to students at the bachelor's degree level and in a particular field of study, such as business, with a particular pedagogy. In order to provide an understanding of the performance of the industry, we would like to identify the fundamental dimensions of product differentiation and the forces motivating and constraining them.

The conduct of institutions of higher education is influenced by long-standing traditions and norms. Some colleges and universities have formal mechanisms for cooperating to share facilities or programs. In addition, the system of transferring credits from one college to another is an important form of cooperation. During some periods of time, institutions cooperated to raise prices or synchronize financial aid awards. These cooperative behaviors are noteworthy and we mention them where appropriate, but in the remainder of this book, we focus much more on the behavior of institutions as they compete for students, faculty, and financial resources. In the next chapter we describe the basic ways institutions of higher education compete for revenue.

Notes

1. A standard assumption of industry studies is that the objective of firms is to maximize profit.
2. There are other revenue streams available to colleges and universities, most notably from ancillary enterprises such as hospitals and medical centers. We do not include such sources in our analyses, although we acknowledge that they may be significant.
3. This total excludes government spending for research.
4. There are several reasons that we compute net, rather than gross, revenues. In contrast to subsidies applied to the institutions' core activities, it is very rare for institutions to subsidize these ancillary enterprises. In addition, separate budgeting for hospitals, auxiliary enterprises, and independent operations makes it easy to identify these costs. We do not subtract costs associated with the production of revenues from sales and services or royalties.

5.   There are other ways to deal with such information asymmetry. For example, the government can regulate the industry, the providers can develop standards or codes of ethics and monitor themselves, or the legal system can serve as a disciplinary device. Reputation can also play an important role in protecting underinformed consumers. Weisbrod does not argue that nonprofits are the best way to deal with these informational asymmetries. He notes that, "given the imperfections of every form of institution, it is good to have variety. Competition among forms of institution is desirable, just as is competition among private firms" (p. 45).

6.   One can derive a formal version of this principle as a direct consequence of the microeconomic theory of not-for-profit enterprises (Hopkins and Massy 1981; James and Rose-Ackerman 1986). Previous research suggests several possible objectives for nonprofits. For example, schools may be *satisficing* (satisfying the demands of multiple constituencies simultaneously), maximizing utility (which may be a function of numerous different factors), minimizing costs or maximizing revenues. These are not necessarily mutually exclusive; see James (1990) and Garvin (1980) for a discussion.

7.   In economic terms we are assuming a clearly identifiable production function. This is a simplification which assists our analysis. It is important to note that this notion of basic operating costs is a theoretical construct in nonprofit organizations which is likely to be below the operating costs actually reported by the institution.

8.   Colleges and universities are formally *accredited* periodically by national or regional organizations. Accrediting agencies are certified by the Department of Education if they are deemed to be reliable authorities on what constitutes quality education or training in institutions of higher education. Accrediting agencies evaluate institutions on the basis of standards of performance that they associate with a sound educational program. These standards vary by type of program and type of institution (see GAO 1996a).

3

Characterizing Institutional
Position and Strategies

Despite voluminous research on higher education, very little attention has been paid to the strategies pursued by institutions in this industry. Institutions of higher education are normally viewed as a "black box" into which resources flow and out of which various products such as degrees or research are generated. Like most large organizations, institutions of higher education have strategies. As a basic definition, a *strategy* means to set goals, make plans for achieving them, and set indicators or benchmarks to assess achievement of these goals. Such a strategy is instrumental in allowing an institution to meet its underlying objective of profit or revenue maximization. Identifying institutional strategies helps us understand the ways the sector as a whole operates and responds to changes in its operating environment.

In this chapter we present a concise description of the institutional behavior we observed in our site visits. Again, we stress that we did not embark upon the site visits with any prior assumptions about the essential components of institutional strategy, although we did have a set of guiding questions based on the industry approach that structured our investigation. We developed the conceptual framework only as an attempt to place the comments we heard from the interviewees into a coherent pattern. We considered a number of other frameworks but judged that the one we present here best fits the data.

Institutions make myriad decisions on which markets to serve and what services to offer in each market. This chapter develops ways of classifying institutional position and important strategic decisions. As we make clear, an understanding of an institution's current posi-

tion as well as its investment strategy is vital to establishing a classification system.

Overview

As noted in the introductory chapter, in order to learn something
about the strategies pursued by institutions of higher education and
their market positions, we conducted a series of site visits at a wide
variety of colleges and universities around the country. A description of the methodology and aggregate information about the sites
can be found in the appendix. During these site visits, we conducted
individual interviews with the president, the senior academic officer,
and the senior financial officer of each institution. In addition, we
interviewed other administrators of the institution, faculty, and students, often in groups. We asked them about the goals of the institution, the plans it had for achieving those goals, how progress toward
the goals was measured, and general perceptions of market conditions. We had no description or set of assumptions about institutional strategies prior to our visits, merely a set of questions motivated by the industry approach. Although the protocols varied slightly
for different interviews, the basic questions asked about the mission
and goals of the instruction, its market niche, which groups have
influence on the institution and in what ways, conflicts among groups,
financial health of the institution and how it is measured, and other
means of measuring outcomes remained the same. For students we
especially asked why they wanted to attend college in general and
why this particular school as opposed to others they had examined.
The basic questions are reproduced in the appendix.

As we completed each site visit, one of us summarized the interviews in a template covering the major industry study elements. This
template required that we document any printed materials and data
supplied by each college or university, such as budgets or strategic
plans. The template asked for a physical description of the campus
and its setting, campus life, the goals of the institution and challenges facing it, planning, measurement and evaluation, description,
and positioning in major markets i.e., students, faculty, government,
sponsored research, gifts, and endowments. The template also required information on the key cost elements of the institution and
any past or potential transformations in the institution. We classified
transformations as those that tend to support existing missions ver-

sus those that required changes to pursue new missions. The appendix contains the whole template.

We developed the conceptual framework only as an attempt to place the comments we heard from the interviewees into a coherent pattern. We considered a number of frameworks and the three authors read these site visit documents to develop independent judgments on various elements of institutional strategy, such as degree offerings or scope. Two concepts emerged as crucial to understanding both the institutions' current position and their strategy. These concepts are *reputation* and *prestige.*

Defining Reputation and Prestige

Reputation and prestige are assets that allow institutions of higher education to convey nonprice information to customers. Higher education institutions can invest in building both reputation and prestige, although some institutions choose to invest primarily in one or the other. The information conveyed by reputation and prestige allows customers to evaluate better the extent to which the institution will be able to satisfy their demands. Such information assets play a role in a number of industries, particularly in markets where the quality of the good or service is difficult for a customer to assess beforehand. Whereas a customer can inspect a shirt and determine whether it is well made and whether it fits before buying it, quality is much more difficult to assess for products and services such as those produced by the higher education industry, where the quality is evaluated either while or after the product or service is consumed. Because the actual benefits of higher education to individuals (e.g., higher lifetime wages) and society (e.g., more productive citizens, lower crime rate) are realized only after years or even decades, the nonprice information conveyed through reputation and prestige plays a particularly important role in this industry.

Reputation can be good or bad, and it is directly related to an institution's ability to meet consistently some set of relatively specific customer demands.[1] Although customers cannot evaluate the quality of the goods and services before they purchase and/or consume them, they can evaluate the quality quickly thereafter. In these situations, reputation can be built through word of mouth based on information from people who have used the product or experienced the service, or on evidence from the provider on the quality of the service provided. For example, some students pursue higher education for the purpose of obtaining a certain type of job. Although prospective students cannot tell whether they will actually get a job if they attend that institution, they can consider the institution's job placement rate, or talk to former students about their job search experiences. The information conveyed through reputation is updated frequently—prospective students will look at job placement rates from recent years not those from ten years ago. An institution's reputation is based on its ability to respond to the demands of customers and demonstrate that it is meeting those demands. This type of reputation for customer satisfaction is what we mean when we use the term *reputation* throughout this volume.

The other nonprice asset, prestige, is always positive, and its source is more intangible. Institutions possessing a high level of prestige often cannot demonstrate that they have met identifiable customer needs. What they can demonstrate is the acquisition of things that tend to be associated with exceptionally high-quality service. If the quality of the service cannot be fully assessed for a long time after the service is performed, or if that quality cannot be easily demonstrated, consumers often develop alternative mechanisms for determining from which provider they should purchase the good or service. Essentially, customers do this by developing a general sense of the institutions that have done a good job over some period of time and then identifying their key characteristics. These might include the range of activities supported by the institution, aspects of its physical infrastructure, the nature of its production process, or the type of customers it serves. Identification of the "best" providers may be based purely on the opinion of customer, or may also be based on the insights of the producers themselves or industry experts.

On the basis of this information on the "best" providers, customers develop images of the features of good service providers. Certain characteristics of a college or university become associated with good providers even though these characteristics are not directly related to the quality of the output. For example, it may be observed that good schools tend to have sports teams and impressive buildings with ivy-covered walls. A rule of thumb is developed that suggests that a high-quality, broad education can be obtained at institutions that have sports teams and ivy-covered walls.[2] Institutions operating in these markets thus develop a strong reputation by "looking right," rather than directly meeting the primary demands of customers.[3] As a result, institutions operating in such markets tend to become very inward looking—focused on acquiring the trappings of the most prestigious institutions in the industry. We identify this as *prestige* in order to distinguish it from reputation. The theory we develop here posits that prestige is built in three specific market activities, which we call the *prestige generators*. They are student quality, research, and sports; we treat each of them in more detail below.

Reputation and prestige are assets that belong to an institution and are built through investment over time. The amount of each asset that an institution possesses at any given time is referred to as the stock of that asset. Prestige and reputation are not absolute concepts. An institution's stock of reputation and prestige can be specific to its choices of which markets to operate in. For example, a specialized art college may have high prestige among bachelor's degree granting art schools. However, if compared with research universities, that same institution would be deemed to have little prestige because it does not engage in research activities.

Because reputation is built on the basis of information that can be obtained quickly, it is less expensive and time consuming to build. With no additional investment, stocks of both reputation and prestige will erode over time. Anecdotal evidence and historical experience suggest that reputation stock erodes more quickly than prestige stock—in large part because consumers can reevaluate an institution's reputation based on new information more frequently. If an institution develops a reputation for placing students in good jobs year after year but then has a terrible job placement rate relative to similar schools one year, this will have an immediate negative effect on the institution's reputation. On the other hand, in the higher education industry prestige appears to be enduring. One reason is that outcomes are only observed after a long period of time, if at all. Moreover, an institution's prestige today often influences its prestige tomorrow. This is, in part, due to the nature of many existing measures of prestige. For example, the *U.S. News and World Report* rankings[4] of colleges and universities allocates a full 25 percent of the total score used to rank institutions to the results of a survey of school presidents, deans, and admissions directors that asks them to rank institutions roughly similar to their own.[5] As a result, there are positive feedbacks in the creation of prestige whereby institutions that are prestigious today are more likely to have a high level of prestige tomorrow. The rankings or ratings of the top schools by *Barron's, U.S. News, Peterson's*, and others reflect a substantial amount of inertia.

Figure 3.1 shows some very general contrasts between reputation and prestige, which can help distinguish prestige from reputation in an institution. Prestige is what economists call a *rival good*, one wherein one individual's (or institution's) consumption of a unit of a good precludes another from enjoying that particular unit. A *nonrival good*, by contrast, is one that can be enjoyed by many consumers without substantially diminishing the value to any one of them. Oil, for example is a rival good, since consuming a barrel of oil means that no one else can also consume that same barrel. The atmosphere, at least for some purposes, is an example of nonrival good, since many people can breathe at the same time without diminishing each other's use of the good. Prestige and reputation, at least approximately, have these divergent characters. Prestige is largely a rival good, meaning that one institution's increase in prestige comes at the expense of others' opportunity to build or maintain their prestige. Reputation, in contrast, can be increased by many institutions at the same time without necessarily competing reputation. This difference stems from the fact that prestige is based on relative, rather than absolute, measurement. Closely related is the notion that accumulating prestige is a zero-sum game. When one institution rises in the rankings, whether in terms of student selectivity, research, or sports, another will fall in the same rankings, at least in the short term. In the longer term, the overall stock of prestige is linked to the number of highly qualified students, the amount of research funding, and the public's appetite for intercollegiate sports competition.

Figure 3.1
Characteristics of the Stocks of Prestige and Reputation

Stock of Prestige	Stock of Reputation
Measured relative to others	Measured in absolute terms
Defined by faculty and insider desires	Defined by customer desires
Depreciates slowly	Depreciates rapidly
A rival good	A non-rival good
Zero-sum game	Positive-sum game

If these increase or decrease, the amount of prestige available from the appropriate prestige generator will change accordingly.

A final observation about the difference between prestige and reputation is that they are generally defined by reference to quite different stakeholder interests. Reputation, by definition, is defined in relation to customer desires for the institution's services. Prestige, on the other hand, is defined in relation to three specific markets, but not necessarily because of the power of the customers in those markets. In a general sense, it is the interests of insiders within the institutions that align with the pursuit of prestige. We summarize this as "faculty and insider desires" in Figure 3.1, but these may take a variety of forms. In some institutions strong administrators may be pursuing prestige with or without faculty approval; in others faculty interests may govern the pursuit of prestige. A final distinction, mentioned earlier, is that prestige depreciates or erodes slowly, over a period of decades, whereas reputation depreciates much more rapidly.

Investing in Reputation and Prestige

As we will illustrate in the next chapter, reputation is often built in narrow market segments, so that investments in reputation need to be relevant to specific external constituencies. Emphasizing curriculum development, especially the development of educational programs that have high relevance to employment, is one option. Fulfilling customer service needs, such as providing education at work sites or designing schedules to match the time adult students have available after work or on weekends, is another option. Because of their fairly specific, limited nature, most investments in reputation are smaller than investments in prestige. In addition, customer needs change over time for almost any customer group, so flexibility is warranted when investing for reputation.

In contrast to the wide range of investments in reputation, investments in prestige are targeted to three major areas, the prestige generators: student quality, research, and sports. Selectivity in admitting students has long been associated with prestige in higher education. A prestigious institution is able to attract many applicants for admission. If it has sufficient income, it can offer generous financial aid and admit the students that the institution desires most. Institutions with less financial capability must admit some of their students with a view toward who can pay the tuition. For institutions that focus on undergraduate education, the primary opportunity to build and maintain prestige is through selectivity in admissions.

For institutions with research emphasis, sponsorship of research is the major opportunity to build or maintain prestige. Attracting research funding requires major investments. An institution must have top-quality faculty and facilities in order to compete in national competitions for research sponsorship. To enhance their competitive positions with respect to research, universities generally offer programs of graduate education to the Ph.D. level. Attracting research faculty, building research facilities, and operating graduate education programs are all expensive investments.

Competitive sports teams can also bring prestige. Sports teams generate revenues directly through ticket sales, television contracts, and merchandising. In addition, successful sports teams generate name recognition for the school, which may spill over into other areas, such as the market for student enrollment, public fiscal support, or private giving. Institutions invest in physical facilities to develop a sports program. Men's football and basketball programs can confer prestige, especially if the teams rank high in national competition. Because football teams require a much larger number of players, staff, and facilities, it is expensive for many institutions to pursue prestige through investments in football. Larger institutions are able to afford the 70 or so scholarships and sizable stadiums that NCAA Division IA teams need. Requirements for basketball are easier. In basketball, smaller institutions can field teams with less strain on their budgets.

The quality of faculty has been proposed as a prestige generator. Faculty quality contributes to institutional prestige. But our framework considers the quality of faculty as one of several means for an institution to compete for prestige, along with the quality of the institution's research equipment and buildings. While a high-quality faculty certainly aids recruitment of students and attracting research funding, faculty represents expenditures rather than revenue. We find it preferable to analyze the three prestige generators that are linked directly to the institution's external customers: student quality, research funding, and sports teams. We therefore do not include faculty quality among our prestige generators, although, obviously, investments in talented faculty are a major means of seeking prestige in both the student and research markets.

The opportunities for investment in prestige in the three areas of student quality, research, and sports are limited, so there is a great deal of similarity in investment patterns across institutions. Investments in reputation, on the other hand, can take many forms, since they tend to address relatively narrow needs in the markets.

To describe institutional strategy, we begin by documenting an institution's investment choices. For each prestige generator—student quality, research, and sports—we note whether an institution is pursuing a strategy of investing in prestige, not investing in prestige, or not operating at all. By the definition of our industry, all institutions must operate in the market for students, so in Figure 3.2 the student row admits only two choices: investing in prestige or not investing in prestige. The other two rows admit the additional possibility of not operating at all in research or sports.

Institutions make much more nuanced choices than merely investing in prestige or not, or participating or not, in these three crucial markets. For students, institutions decide which degrees to offer and in which subjects. For research, the relevant variables are the type of funding (federal, other government, industrial, etc.), the character of research, and the fields of inquiry. For sports, again there are level and breadth considerations, such as, in which NCAA leagues to participate and in which sports to field teams. All of these multi-dimensional choices are represented in our three-dimensional version of Figure 3.2, shown as Figure 3.3. That figure is meant to suggest that in each of the three markets institutions choose whether to participate, whether to pursue prestige, and at which level and breadth.

Figure 3.2
Strategic Choices in the Three Prestige Generators

	Investing in Prestige	Not Investing in Prestige	Not Operating
Students			
Research			
Sports			

Figure 3.3
More Complete Strategic Choices for Students, Research, and Sports

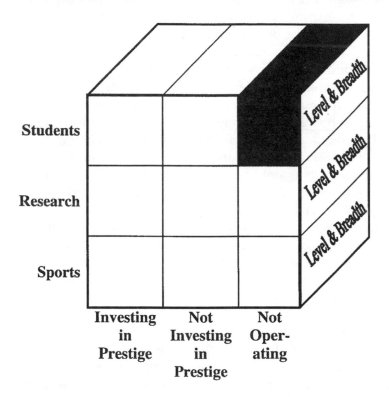

In practice there are potential ambiguities in assigning a specific institution's choices to investments in reputation or investments in prestige. If the investment does not concern one of the three prestige generators, we know it is an investment in reputation. Within the three crucial markets, Table 3.1 gives a guide to typical investments that are associated with prestige, as opposed to reputation. In addition, it is important to know whether an institution possesses a stock of prestige. To help in making that determination, Table 3.1 also gives a guide to measuring prestige in the three crucial markets.

If an institution possesses prestige in at least one of these three markets, we say that it possesses prestige. If an institution is investing in prestige in at least one of these three markets, we say that it is investing in prestige. We do not provide a detailed guide to judging investments in reputation or measuring reputation, but note that every other institutional activity that is connected to an *external* cus-

Table 3.1
Identifying Investments and Measuring Prestige in the Prestige Generators

Prestige
Generator

Specific Investments Measures of Prestige

	Specific Investments	Measures of Prestige
Students	Merit scholarships Faculty Classroom and dorm facilities	High SAT/ACT scores Admissions selectivity *U.S. News* rankings
Research	Faculty with research record Laboratories and facilities	Volume of federal grants National Research Council rankings
Sports	Player scholarships Highly-paid coaches Stadiums/arenas	AP, USA Today/ESPN, and other national rankings and polls Bowl games, tournaments, Olympic medals

tomer is a candidate for investing in reputation. The next chapter offers many illustrations of reputation in each of the four revenue markets.

With these definitions, we are now ready to define the basic strategic types we will use throughout this book. Assignment of a strategic type depends, in principle, upon an institution's present stock of prestige and reputation as well as its current investment in prestige and reputation. There are various considerations to weigh in assigning strategic types. For different analytical purposes, modifications to the taxonomy are appropriate. We present two variants of the taxonomy, the first one grouping all institutions into three types then a modification allowing for an additional type. We also mention other ways that the taxonomy can be extended.

In the Tables 3.2 and 3.3, we use a logical truth table style to define the mapping from the stock and investments to the strategic type. Table 3.2 shows a fundamental way of assigning strategic types. The first row indicates that an institution with high current prestige (denoted H) is called P, or prestigious, regardless of any of its choices in the other variables. An institution without high prestige (i.e., moderate or low prestige) but with at least moderate current investments in prestige is called PS, or prestige-seeking. Institutions that do not fall into either of these categories (i.e., moderate or low prestige and

Table 3.2
Summarizing Institutional Strategy and Position in Three Types

| Prestige | | Reputation | | |
Stock	Investments	Stock	Investments	Strategic Type
H	*	*	*	P
M L	H M	*	*	PS
M L	L	*	*	R

Notes: H=high, M=moderate, and L=low for stocks and investments. * Indicates that any value qualifies. P=Prestigious, PS=Prestige-seeking, and R=Reputation-based for strategic types.

low investment in prestige) are called R, or reputation-based. Note that R institutions may have any amount of reputation or any level of investment in reputation.

For some purposes, it would be useful to characterize R institutions further, along the lines of P and PS institutions. We could define reputation-building, reputation-maintaining, and reputation-declining institutions based on whether they were investing enough in reputation to maintain, increase, or fail to maintain their current level of reputation. But we will not focus on this taxonomy because the level of reputation does not define the character of an institution to the same extent that prestige does, since reputation decays or depreciates much more rapidly. If an institution does not continually invest in reputation, its reputation will erode. The same is not true for a P institution, which will maintain prestige for a long time.

There is a modification related to reputation that we will introduce, although it complicates the taxonomy. Although the formal taxonomy in Table 3.2 does not imply that PS institutions are failing to invest strongly in reputation, that is a natural conclusion from the way we have classified strategic types. Institutions pursuing prestige typically have a substantial reputation in one or more areas. Some prestige seekers do erode their reputations in order to generate funds for investments in prestige. Other PS institutions have largely self-sufficient reputation-based programs that make substantial investments in maintaining a high reputation and may or may not generate cash to fuel prestige seeking. Table 3.3 formalizes this notion by separating additional cases that we call PS-R hybrids because they have two distinct components: a PS component and an R component. As we explain a bit later, the institu-

Table 3.3
Summarizing Institutional Strategy and Position (with Hybrids)

| Prestige | | Reputation | | |
Stock	Investments	Stock	Investments	Strategic Type
H	*	*	*	P
M L	H M	M L	*	PS
M L	H M	*	L	PS
M L	L	*	*	R
M L	H M	H	H M	PS-R hybrid

Notes: H=high, M=moderate, and L=low for stocks and investments. * Indicates that any value qualifies. P=Prestigious, PS=Prestige-seeking, and R=Reputation-based for strategic types. PS-R hybrid is a hybrid institution encompassing both strategic types PS and R.

tions that have this hybrid character have separate physical campus facilities and faculties for their PS and R programs, although the definition here does not require that separation. To qualify, an institution must otherwise be a PS type and have a program with a high reputation and a high or moderate investment in reputation. An institution with a low investment in reputation is classified as a regular PS type because the institution is avoiding investment in reputation in favor of investments in prestige.

We have described a number of measurements of current position, investment behavior, and market participation. Sometimes it will be necessary to go into the full depth of description, as we have above. For many purposes, however, a more concise description of institutional position and strategy will suffice. We present one such simplification in the form of a cube run in Figure 3.4.

The first dimension of an institution's position and strategy is reflected in the highest *degree* offered with regularity, from associate's degree to Ph.D. The second dimension of strategy is reflected by the *scope* of the institution's activities, ranging from narrow to broad. This variable is actually an aggregation of a number of dimensions, including those in Figure 3.2 and others: disciplinary breadth, generality of the educational environment, geographic focus of the institution, etc. The final strategic dimension is the *strategic type* from Table 3.3, which is a concise description of the institution's stocks of prestige and reputation and its investment in prestige and reputation.

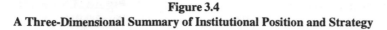

Figure 3.4
A Three-Dimensional Summary of Institutional Position and Strategy

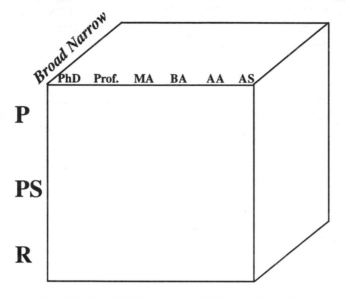

Institutional Mission and Degree Level
Do Not Determine Strategic Type

Our framework allows for the three strategic types, P, PS, and R, to be found among many different sorts of institutions. In particular, all universities are not prestigious, and all community colleges are not reputation-based. Many of the nation's most familiar universities are prestigious because of some combination of achievement in research, student quality, and sports. (Again all three prestige generators are not required for an institution to be called prestigious.) We visited a community college that we classified as prestigious because it had built a strong name brand and drew students from a much wider geographic area than do most other two-year institutions. In general, this community college possessed prestige in the sense that all of its activities benefited from its strong general market position. Conversely, many broad universities have little prestige. They are focused on serving specific needs among students, industry, and employers.

Institutional Resource Allocation

A fundamental decision facing institutions is how to allocate any discretionary revenue among investment in reputation, investment in prestige, savings, and extra consumption. Figure 3.5 depicts the basic dynamics of institutional strategy. Investment in reputation contributes to an institution's stock of reputation; investment in prestige, to the stock of prestige; and savings, to the size of the endowment. Endowment is just the industry's term for the institution's savings account. The endowment generates direct financial returns for the institution, increasing net revenue in the future. Reputation and prestige benefit the institution by improving its ability to generate revenue in the four key revenue markets. This revenue generating ability, in turn, determines the level of future discretionary resources and, hence, the future resource allocation process.

Consumption refers to the use of resources in a manner that benefits internal constituents rather than customers of the industry. From an accounting perspective, consumption often looks like an operating cost in a nonprofit institution. Consumption can take a variety of forms, depending on the control structure within the institution. For example, administrators, faculty and staff benefit from things such as above-market wages, lower teaching loads, smaller class sizes, high-quality research facilities, or recreational facilities. In for-profit institutions, there is another important internal stakeholder, the shareholders or owners, who receive consumption in the form of increased value of their holdings or a dividend payout. Some consumption

Figure 3.5
Dynamics of Institutional Strategy

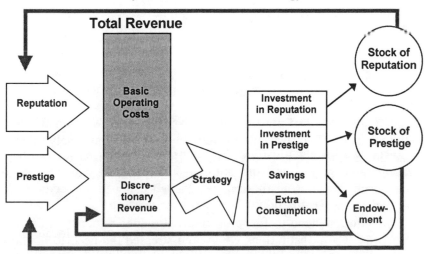

opportunities overlap with investments in reputation and prestige. For example, high-quality facilities both advance institutional reputation or prestige and also contribute to the satisfaction of those faculty, students, and administrators who use them. The diagram in Figure 3.5 labels a quantity "extra consumption" to denote those expenditures of discretionary resources that generate consumption without also acting as investments in reputation or prestige. For the remainder of this book, we will use the term "*consumption*" to denote total consumption, including the consumption value of investments in reputation and prestige as well as any extra consumption.

Resources allocated to savings are those that increase the level of the endowment. Institutions can also engage in reverse saving if they take money from the endowment to cover basic operating costs, for consumption, or to invest in reputation or prestige.

Finally, institutions may invest discretionary resources in reputation or prestige. What motivates institutions to invest in reputation or prestige? As in other industries, reputation and prestige essentially provide firms with a buffer from competitive forces; prestige allows them to distinguish themselves from many other providers, thereby allowing them to attract more customers or to charge a higher price for their services. In the higher education environment, there are market segments in which reputation has stronger payoffs relative to prestige and those in which prestige has stronger payoffs relative to reputation. In general, institutions can increase discretionary resources, which can then be spent on consumption, if they are able to acquire a high level of prestige in a lucrative segment of a market. This opportunity provides some institutions with an incentive to invest in prestige.

Overall Comparison of P, PS, R, and PS-R Hybrid Type Institutions

Now that we have defined the stocks of prestige and reputation and given an overview of institutional positions and investment choices, we further illustrate the institutional types by using observations and quotations from our site visits. Recall that we categorized each of the 26 institutions we visited using the procedures described in the appendix.

P institutions tend to focus on internal values rather than external standards. The P institutions we visited stressed the need to maintain excellence or continue to improve the quality of what they do. This inward focus is reflected in goals such as "to be the best in whatever we do," "to continue to deliver a quality liberal arts education into the 21st century," "to maintain excellence and quality," and "to solidify our position as a top university nationally and internationally."

P schools tend to define themselves by the specific set of activities in which they are engaged and are confident that customers will be drawn to them because of their perceived excellence in those areas. Put another way, they are not actively engaged in building a market for their services or increasing the number of potential customers but in vying for a growing share of a market that already exists.

Because the measures of prestige are derived from features of institutions that currently have a high level of prestige, investment in prestige is conservative. Prestige is not built through major innovation. While P colleges and universities can and do make changes or additions to their curriculum or activity mix in response to changes in the environment, these tend to be marginal, leveraging their investment in prestige in one area to build or develop another area or developing clearly subordinate activities to generate revenue in support of fundamental processes.

P institutions are buffered from the environment because of their prestige, but they cannot ignore external pressure. Institutions face continual challenges to their prestige, not only from changes in the environment but also from other institutions that would like to improve their own position in the higher education pecking order. A delicate balancing act is required to maintain prestige and, hence, glean the associated rewards. For example, federal research money flows to institutions known for high-quality research, and those funds are necessary to maintain the quality of the research as well as prestige. Similarly, institutions generally need academic prestige in order to attract a large number of applicants so that they can be selective in admissions; however, they need to be selective to get that prestige.

PS institutions do not currently have a high level of prestige but would like to. Their primary resource allocation strategy is to invest in building prestige. These schools are working to increase their prominence, or "to become a university of hemispheric importance," "to improve our national reputation," "to be one of the top ten private universities." They are less likely to define their goals in relation to what they currently do or to what their customers need than to what P institutions currently do. Indeed, their goal statements often include references to specific P institutions. Administrators at one such institution said that their goal was to be "like Cal Tech, only more broad." Several public PS institutions expressed a goal of being more like the flagship institution in the state. In spite of the perceived deficiencies in existing measures, the PS types are fixated on these relative measures of excellence and prestige. Indeed, prestige-seeking institutions compare themselves to other institutions on almost any dimension for which there are data, and even offer comparisons on dimensions for which there are no data. One PS institution noted that it is better than Harvard and Stanford at the character development of students. Many have two different sets of comparison groups, a "peer group" that reflects the schools they are most like and an "aspiration group" that reflects those they are striving to become like.

Recognizing that they do not have prestige in any particular area, PS institutions are not as constrained by their current set of activities as P institutions. Instead, they are investing in a set of activities, some of which might propel them to a position of national or regional prominence. It is worth stressing that these activities will improve their prestige in the higher education industry and can be quite different from those that meet the needs of their current constituents. They are choosing this set of activities in order to allow themselves to develop the highest prestige possible.

P and PS institutions operate in markets with few objective measurement criteria and, as a result, make heavy use of subjective quality benchmarks. The most prestigious institutions form the basis for these yardsticks and act as leaders in market segments where imitation rather than innovation is the key to a strong position. When asked how they know whether they are achieving their goals, both P and PS institutions reported that they focus on comparative measures of performance. They are acutely aware of *U.S. News and World Report* rankings and use this as a measure of prestige. Institutions engaged in research activities measure the level of federal research funding they receive and compare that with what is received by other institutions. The Carnegie Classification, which is discussed later in this chapter, is another important measure of prestige, and for many institutions fulfilling the requirements for a "higher" Carnegie Classification rank is a primary short-term goal. Some institutions examine the National Research Council rankings, the number of awards won by faculty or alumni, and a host of input measures (such as SAT scores of incoming freshmen collected nationally by the College Board).

R institutions have not accumulated a high level of prestige; neither are they investing in acquiring it. Instead, these institutions are focused on meeting the identifiable demands of customers. These schools describe their goals in relation to the needs of external constituents. The specific identity of the latter constituents depends on the nature of the institution and its level of specialization but is most frequently some identifiable student population or community group. The constituents have relatively clear demands, the satisfaction of which is fairly easy to measure. For example, students might want a bachelor's degree, a job-related skill, or a job. A state might want to provide its residents with access to the institution. Because reputation is built by successfully meeting customer demands at a reasonable price, as opposed to meeting the (often process-oriented) expectations of internal groups, R institutions tend to be student centered, dynamic, and responsive to the changing needs of society.

This external focus is most clearly reflected in the goal expressed by an interviewee at one institution "to become the best in a new class of urban universities: an institution which is judged by the education level of its constituency, and for which there is a seamless barrier between the university and the community." An interviewee at another, more specialized, institution articulated the goal of providing access to higher education for adult students who are not being served by traditional institutions. R institutions specialize primarily in the needs of a population rather than the subjects taught or type of research conducted.

Because they are motivated by a desire to serve certain customers rather than meet some subjective standards that contribute to prestige in the higher education environment, these institutions can be innovative in terms of educational delivery. For example, one institution serving independently motivated adult learners with some experience in higher education is purely an external degree program with no residency requirement. This college has no full-time faculty and hires faculty from other schools on a consulting basis to help with program development, serve on academic advisory committees, and evaluate degree proposals. Several of the R institutions we visited do not have a traditional campus with impressive buildings, but, rather, provide instruction in conveniently located office buildings. Some of the R institutions that do have a main campus are focusing on growth in remote locations that are more convenient for potential students or that allow them to expand access without building new facilities.

Not surprisingly, R institutions are much less concerned with rankings and other prestige measures. To the extent they use comparison groups, it is to compare faculty salaries or to engage in cost benchmarking. Many of these institutions had developed or were in the process of developing measures to help them evaluate the impact of their activities on students or on the community. When asked how they evaluate their performance, interviewees at these institutions commonly mentioned alumni satisfaction surveys, postgraduation success of students, and the educational level of the population at large. Administrators at one institution suggested that the tools that they need to evaluate progress toward their goals are not available but that they are involved in an intensive effort to develop them.

In addition to institutions representing the three basic types of institution, we observed two PS-R hybrid institutions, each of which had clearly defined PS and R components. Reinforcing the notion that the market segments in which prestige is important are distinct from those in which reputation is key is the observation that institutions pursuing both prestige-seeking and reputation-based strategies do so through clearly distinguished, separate entities that engage in different types of activities. For example, one "hybrid" institution we visited makes a clear distinction between the undergraduate college and the law school (which are clearly PS entities) and the graduate programs (which are R entities). This institution had essentially been operating the graduate programs at a profit, and these profits were used to support prestige-building activities in the undergraduate college and law school. Interestingly, the institution is planning to cease these cross-subsidies and put "every tub on its own bottom." And although the two segments of the institution do not share faculty or even a campus, the prestige of the college and law school seems to improve the revenue generating ability of the graduate programs. Much could be learned about the costs and benefits of P, PS, and R strategies through a more in-depth study of hybrid institutions. The practice of P and PS institutions developing "high-margin," customer-oriented programs appears to be increasingly popular among institutions of higher education, and the implications of such activities are not well understood.

The Carnegie Classification

Although we may be the first to use the terms *prestige* and *reputation* in this specific way others have wrestled with defining similar concepts. The dominant classification system for institutions among those who study higher education has been the Carnegie Classification. Because of its importance, we discuss this system first and then turn to other systems in the next section.

The Carnegie Classification was originally intended as a system of descriptive categories with which to group broadly similar institutions for research projects. Nonetheless, these categories have taken on the practical meaning of ladders of prestige. Table 3.4 displays the definitions used in this system in 1994. The Carnegie Foundation for the Advancement of Teaching has revised the definitions since they were first developed in 1973. Some of the revisions were merely to adjust numerical measures for inflation, like federal research funding. Other revisions were renaming categories and changing measures used to classify institutions.

In terms of the practical meaning in the field of higher education, the classification has established a ladder for institutions to climb. In undergraduate institutions, focus on the liberal arts ranks higher than focus on other disciplines. Greater selectivity in admissions ranks higher than less selectivity. For institutions that grant the doctorate degree, those with more Ph.D. programs and larger federal research funding occupy a higher status. (We will refrain from saying that the classification establishes a strict hierarchy reading down the major categories than those with fewer programs and less funding making research universities superior to liberal arts colleges, although some within higher education certainly feel that such a hierarchy exists.)

The perception of this hierarchy, at least within research institutions and undergraduate colleges, echoes our concept of prestige. The classification quantifies the single most important prestige measure for research and for undergraduate students. The classification then makes the simplifying determination that, for research institutions, only research prestige matters.

Table 3.4
The 1994 Carnegie Classification Criteria

Carnegie Classification	Criteria
Research Universities I	50 or more doctorates per year, and $40 million or more per year in federal research support
Research Universities II	50 or more doctorates per year, and $15.5–40 million per year in federal research support
Doctoral Universities I	40 or more doctorates per year across at least 5 disciplines
Doctoral Universities II	10 or more doctorates per year across at least 3 disciplines, or 20 or more doctorates per year total
Master's (Comprehensive) Colleges and Universities I	40 or more master's degrees per year across at least 3 disciplines
Master's (Comprehensive) Colleges and Universities II	20 or more master's degrees per year overall
Baccalaureate (Liberal Arts) Colleges I	40 percent or more of bachelor's degrees in liberal arts fields, and restrictive in admissions
Baccalaureate Colleges II	Less than 40 percent of bachelor's degrees in liberal arts fields, or less restrictive in admissions
Associate of Arts Colleges	Associate's and certificate programs and, with few exceptions, no bachelor's degrees
Specialized Institutions	At least half of all degrees awarded in a single discipline
Tribal Colleges and Universities	Members of the American Indian Higher Education Consortium

Source: Carnegie Foundation (1994).
Note: Enrollments and revenues used to classify institutions were those from the 1989-90 through 1991-92 school years.

We do not view the Carnegie Foundation as having established the categories *for the purpose of measuring prestige*. But two forces are at work. First, the classification attempts to group similar institutions. As our taxonomy makes plain, we view P institutions as being different from other institutions, so measuring prestige in some way is necessary to claim a useful grouping. Second, the industry is hungry for objective—and widely recognized—measures of something so difficult to quantify as prestige. Therefore, the industry has seized on the Carnegie Classification as providing the yardstick for prestige.

The foundation has itself become concerned about the strong meaning attached to its categories among faculty, higher education administrators, and state governments. Even the ostensibly independent *U.S. News* ranking, in fact, sorts institutions into groups based solely on the Carnegie Classification before any other variable is considered.

In response to concerns such as these, the 2000 revision of the Carnegie Classification purposely eliminates most of these status distinctions (Carnegie Foundation 2000). The Carnegie Foundation promises a new classification in 2004 with multiple dimensions for characterizing institutions. The classification measures key aspects of prestige and, indeed, it has itself come to *define* prestige in some arenas. The definitions do not differentiate any measures of reputation and say nothing about an institution's investment behavior regarding either prestige or reputation. Perhaps some of the dimensions to be added by 2004 will further reflect our notions of prestige, reputation, and investment.

Other Definitions of Prestige and Reputation

While the Carnegie Classification has been the most widely used taxonomy for institutions, we are aware of a number of other systems for measuring institutions that involve determinations of what we call prestige and reputation. Like the Carnegie Classification, these other systems measure institutional position rather than investment behavior.

The most common method of measuring institutional position that we observed in our site visits is the comparison of indicators with the average of a set of indicators of institutions. We discussed this above for prestigious and prestige-seeking institutions, but reputation-based institutions use comparison groups as well. The use of comparison groups to measure prestige is somewhat of an art, as it depends crucially on picking an appropriate set of institutions to represent the prestige aspiration.

These comparison groups can also be used to measure investments in reputation and prestige by selecting appropriate indicators of investment for comparison. Some examples include construction of new buildings, faculty salaries, teaching loads, and athletic scholarships.

Zemsky, Shaman, and Iannozzi (1997) have developed a specific classification system for four-year institutions, based on the undergraduate student market. Their classification relies on indicators including the fraction of part-time students and the ratio of degrees to enrollment. They term the most elite institutions *name brand* and the least elite *convenience* to symbolize the major attributes that institutions strive for at the two extremes. Their system essentially measures institutional position, corresponding approximately to our notion of prestige, restricted to the undergraduate student market. They did not develop measures of investment in prestige or reputation, so we would not be able to map institutions onto our framework without these additional pieces of information. This research group has also extended the classification approach to include two-year institutions.

There are existing measurements of prestige in research. The Carnegie Classification has incorporated a simple but powerful standard of exceeding a given threshold in federal research funding. The National Research Council produces more detailed indicators of prestige for many specific disciplines about once a decade. One influential element of that study is a peer survey asking about other departments in the same field. Again, these indicator systems measure position but not investment behavior.

Although we are not aware of a composite index of prestige in intercollegiate athletics, each individual sport certainly has annual rankings that could be combined into an overall rating of institutions, accumulated over a period of time, and included with other candidate measures such as Olympic medals won by students or graduates. As it is with other prestige generators, measuring institutional investments will be much more difficult.

Purely positional systems for specific markets are certainly useful in examining customer decisionmaking in those markets. Although it is difficult, we believe that gaining an understanding of an institution's investment behavior as well as its current position is essential to understanding and analyzing institutional strategy. Strategy necessarily incorporates a sense of motion, specifically intended motion.

Summary

Our work has highlighted the need to understand both an institution's present position, measured in the various markets for higher education, as well as its investment behavior. Based on our site visits we have characterized institutions according to their current stocks of prestige and reputation and their investment behavior. We combined these measures of stock and investment to produce a strategic type for each institution we visited: P, PS, R, or PS-R hybrid. In the remainder of the book, we explore what it means to be an institution of each strategic type as well as the effects of the other elements of an institution's present position and investment behavior.

Notes

1.   When we talk about institutions trying to build a reputation, we assume that it is a good reputation they are striving for.
2.   Customers of the institution are not the only ones who rely on such rules of thumb for attributing quality output on the basis of features of the production process. This is precisely what higher education accreditation agencies do.
3.   Because students associate certain features, such as a high- quality library, with their primary demand, they come to demand those features as well. In this sense institutions are meeting secondary demands of students by acquiring these features.
4.   *U.S. News and World Report* ranks U.S. colleges and universities on an annual basis. Institutions are assigned a score on the basis of a wide variety of factors such as standardized test scores of entering students, student-faculty ratios, and size of the endowment. Using the Carnegie Classification, which we discuss later in this chapter, institutions are then divided into several categories (colleges are distinguished from universities; regional schools are distinguished from national schools) and ranked within their group on the basis of that score.
5.   It would be fascinating to know what factors these individuals use to rank institutions. Such a question might easily be added to a future survey.

4

Institutional Position and Strategy in the Four Key Revenue Markets

The four key markets in which institutions of higher education compete and that generate revenue,—student enrollments, research, public fiscal support, and private giving—all have distinct features. Customer motivation, the determinants of demand, market segmentation, institutional outputs and outcomes for customers, and market signals all have unique characteristics. How does a school's current position, especially its stock reputation and prestige affect its opportunities in each of these markets? How does a school's overall strategy and, in particular, its investments in reputation and prestige, shape its conduct in each of these markets? In this chapter we discuss the institutional positions and strategies of P, PS, and R schools in the context of the four revenue markets. As indicated in the preface, more background detail on each revenue market is provided in Brewer, Gates, and Goldman (2001); here the focus is on resource allocation behavior, and institutions' strategic positioning in these markets.

Student Enrollments

Student enrollments are the reason for the existence of the overwhelming majority of higher education institutions. Almost all colleges and universities consider the teaching of students part of their core mission. Most have teaching as their primary mission, and many are dependent on attracting students and collecting tuition and fee revenues for their survival. The student market is the one market that we do not allow institutions to avoid. From an industry perspective, then, students are the essential customers. The purpose of this section is to understand the ways in which institutions of higher education attract students.

51

The number of students served has grown dramatically in the past 30 years. In 1965, enrollment in higher education in the United States was approximately 6 million—by 1970, it was 8 million, and by 1995, it was approaching 15 million (*Almanac of Higher Education* 1995). The growth in enrollments since 1970 is summarized in Figure 4.1, where the particularly rapid growth in public two-year college enrollments is evident. The industry awarded over a half million associate's degrees, over one million bachelor's degrees, and over a half million graduate degrees in 1995. Figure 4.2 indicates the distribution of these degrees, indicating that the growth has not been uniform in the sector over the past two decades. As the market for educational services has grown, the characteristics of students served by the industry have become more diverse in terms of age, race, gender, socioeconomic status, academic preparation, and academic objectives (American Council on Education 1996). Figure 4.3 shows that the proportion of nonwhite students—especially Hispanic and Asian students—has grown notably. All of these trends indicate that it is the *nontraditional* students who have represented the greatest growth in the market, especially students served by R institutions rather than by P and PS institutions.

Although many people know from an early age that they will pursue higher education, for others the decision to attend college is not so obvious. Potential students must decide whether they will purchase any education service beyond high school and, if so, what type of service and from which institution. In so doing, students compare the benefits they expect to receive from the service with the costs they will incur in obtaining it.[1] The costs of obtaining higher education include not only the "price" of the education (tuition and fees) and associated costs (books, supplies, transportation, etc.) but also non-price factors such as forgone wages (if the student has to cut back on the number of hours worked or quit working entirely) and the cost of effort the student devotes to studying.

In many instances these opportunity costs will exceed the explicit costs of tuition and fees and will be a crucial factor in determining whether a potential student decides to enroll in any institution of higher education. The *value added* by an institution of higher education to the student is equal to the benefit the student derives from the service minus total costs. If the costs involved in pursuing higher education exceed the expected benefits so that the value added is

Figure 4.1
Enrollment in U.S. Higher Education

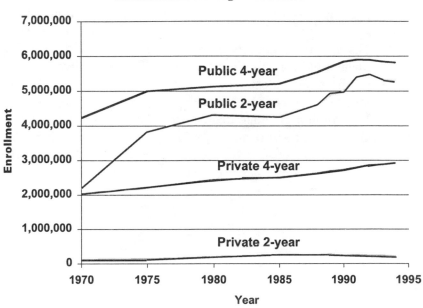

Figure 4.2
Degrees Granted in U.S. Higher Education

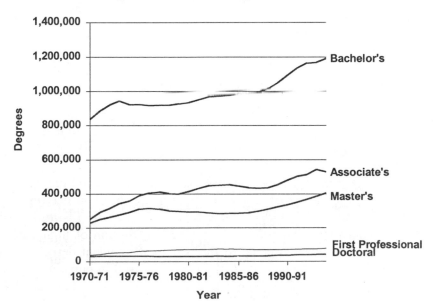

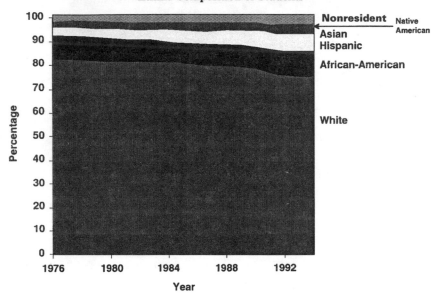

Figure 4.3
Ethnic Composition of Students

negative from the student's perspective, he/she will not enroll in any institution and will therefore not be a customer of the higher education industry. In theory, a student will choose to attend the institution that provides him/her with the most value added. In reality, calculations of value added are difficult to make. Students do not possess perfect information about the stream of costs and benefits of attending college. These streams will be influenced by a wide variety of the things outside of the control the student and the institution (such as the state of the economy or changes in technology) as well as by the actions of the student and the institution. Information about the institution and its ability to meet the needs of certain types of customers can help a student more precisely evaluate the value added from attending a particular school. Price is not a good signal of quality in the student market because for many institutions price bears almost no relation to the actual cost of providing the service. Students rely on reputation and prestige to provide that information. Indeed, as enrollments have risen, so have prices, as shown in Table 4.1. In all categories of institutions, the posted price of tuition has risen faster than the rate of inflation over the past decade.

Table 4.1
Tuition and Fees at Various Categories of Institutions
(Constant 1994 Dollars)

Year	Private University	Private Four-Year College	Public University	Public Four-Year College	Public Two-Year College
1985-86	10,058	7,694	2,095	1,578	874
1986-87	10,828	8,231	2,202	1,665	880
1987-88	11,236	8,421	2,211	1,802	904
1988-89	11,577	8,785	2,261	1,856	894
1989-90	12,089	9,087	2,377	1,879	883
1990-91	12,599	9,289	2,391	1,890	912
1991-92	13,082	9,714	2,586	2,074	1,005
1992-93	13,584	9,920	2,710	2,281	1,067
1993-94	14,006	10,294	2,862	2,401	1,130
1994-95	14,486	10,646	2,948	2,474	1,145

Students derive a wide variety of benefits from higher education and pursue higher education for many different reasons (Pascarella and Terenzini 1991; Astin, Korn, Mahoney, and Sax 1995). It is useful to categorize the benefits into two basic types: immediate consumption and long-term investment benefits. The investment benefits of higher education include increased future earnings potential, economic advancement, intellectual development, social skills development, physical development, specific knowledge, status/recognition, and a credential. These benefits can stem from the actual transfer of knowledge or training (a student learns a specific marketable skill from the institution) or from other value-added activities of the institution, such as a job fair. Students can also benefit from the screening function of the institution (Spence 1973). If it is difficult to gain admission to an institution, then having a degree from that institution sends a signal to potential employers or to society at large that the individual has certain desirable attributes (such as intelligence, discipline, or motivation).

Students also derive consumption benefits from higher education. These benefits include opportunities for socializing, participation in athletic activities, and cultural and sporting events, etc. Students may have widely different preferences regarding different aspects of consumption. Some may want to attend a "party school" where they can spend a minimum amount of time studying and a maximum amount of time socializing with friends. Others may view long nights engaged in philosophical discourse as a form of consumption and look for an institution where such activities dominate the social life. Others might have a strong preference for attending a school far from home, near a beautiful surf spot, or in an urban area rich in cultural opportunities.

To meet this variety of needs, institutions offer a "bundled" service, an array of investment and consumption benefits (for example, a degree, student services, football games, and interesting colleagues) for a particular price. Students purchase the bundle that provides them with the greatest expected benefit net of costs. Students differ dramatically with respect to the weight they place on price as opposed to nonprice factors, on the consumption benefits vs. the investment benefits of higher education, and even on different elements of the consumption and investment benefits. This heterogeneity was reflected in the objectives of students we talked with in our site visits.[2]

Students bring revenue to the institution in which they enroll in the form of tuition and fees. In many states, state and local funding supplements tuition revenue and is based on enrollment, so students indirectly bring government revenue as well. The funds for tuition and fees come not only from the private resources of the student but also from the federal government (through federal tuition grants and interest subsidies for student loans), the state government (through state financial aid programs), and private sources (through scholarship programs) (see Klein, Carroll, Hawes-Dawson, McCaffry, and Robyn 1995). Although the student might not be paying the tuition bill him/herself, the institution must enroll the student in order to acquire the state, federal, or private scholarship money.

Students also have personal attributes that can contribute to the prestige of the institution in which they are enrolled. The relationship between student characteristics and institutional prestige is reflected in the rankings or classifications of colleges and graduate and professional programs by *Barron's*, *Peterson's*, *U.S. News and World Report,* and various other publications. These are based in part on criteria such as average test scores of entering students, the percentage of applicants who are admitted, the institution's yield rate (the proportion of accepted students who decide to attend the institution), and the students' average high school GPA. Through these measures, students become an important element of an institution's prestige.

The fact that higher education is a multidimensional, bundled service and that students have diverse preferences over different aspects of the bundle suggests that there is an opportunity for institutions to serve the needs of students in a variety of ways. In the context of our site visits, we observed such heterogeneity. In particular, we identified a strong distinction between the strategies pursued by R institutions on the one hand and P and PS institutions on the other. The primary reason is that, whereas R institutions are focused on building their reputations by meeting the needs of students, P and PS institutions are focused on improving the selectivity of the admissions process and only secondarily on actually meeting the needs of the students.

The goal of R institutions is normally to maintain or increase the number of students they serve by reaching new student markets. However, they face competition for these students from other institutions in the industry. R institutions can increase the number of students they serve by identifying needs that are not currently being met, by meeting the needs more effectively than other institutions, or by redesigning the bundle of services provided so that it more appropriately reflects the priorities of students. If they do any of these things better than other institutions, they develop strong reputations in the market for students.

Because R institutions are not trying to build prestige, they derive little benefit from the attributes of the student, per se. Instead, students are valued for the revenue they bring into the institution. To the extent that these schools select students, it is on their ability to pay; their ability to benefit from the services of the institution (as evidenced, for example, by their commitment to the program of study); and, in the case of public institutions, their residency status. Because these institutions do not engage in highly selective admission processes, students do not benefit simply from the fact that they were admitted to the institution. Instead, in order to provide benefit to the student, the institution must actually provide a service: generate knowledge, teach the student a skill, or provide the student with consumption benefits.

We observed both highly focused and broad R institutions. The broad R schools offered a wide range of programs (vocational and academic, many subject areas, many degree levels) to a variety of students (full-time and part-time, traditional college age and older students, etc.). An administrator at one R university described it as "the Wal-Mart of higher education"—offering almost every type of program imaginable at a reasonable price. Another broad R university espouses an "if they will come, we will build it" philosophy, it will develop a degree program if it can identify enough people with a common interest. This university offers traditional lecture courses and seminars as well as distance learning and correspondence options. It is starting to develop programs that could be offered right at the work sites of interested individuals. For example, courses for a nursing program are being offered at a local hospital and a psychology degree program for police officers is being held at the police station. Many community colleges offer such "contract" education for employers; in general, the broad R institutions tended to be publicly controlled.

At the other extreme, we observed R schools that are focused on serving a particular type of student (for example, adult learners or part-time students) or offering a focused bundle of services that would appeal to a narrow population (e.g., young people interested in obtaining a job in a particular technical field). These institutions are often targeting needs that were not being well served by the traditional higher education sector. Many of these institutions are focused on adult learners who place little or no value on many of the traditional residential aspects of higher education and place a high value on convenience and an ability to work full time while attending school. One public R college targets adult learners who are highly motivated, have some experience with higher education, need a great deal of flexibility, and are interested primarily in obtaining a degree. This college is an external degree program that has no faculty of its own, offering students credit toward a degree through a variety of mechanisms ranging from formal courses at accredited institutions to standardized tests.

These specialized R institutions experiment with alternative delivery mechanisms and academic structures. For example, one institution offers courses year-round in six-week blocks, allowing students to focus more intensively on fewer subjects. This system also provides students with more convenience, allowing them to take short amounts of time off from school if they need to. Another school develops comprehensive curricula around the skills needed to be successful in identified careers. Rather than taking a generic math course, an English course, and a political science course, students learn these disciplines in a particular context related to the career they are pursuing. A significant amount of planning is required to integrate the academic learning with the applied context.

Although R institutions are frequently disparaged as "degree mills," they are driven to maintain their reputations for meeting customer needs by providing customers with real value. In order to succeed, R institutions must constantly monitor the needs of their customers. For example, one for-profit institution we visited offers highly specialized degree programs designed to help the students achieve specific career aims. This institution's primary measure of success is the extent to which graduating students get jobs in their fields of study. In order to achieve success, the institution spends a lot of time researching the needs of the local business community, student demand, as well as labor market demand. The results drive program offerings and curriculum development activities. Programs in which there is strong demand on the student side but weak demand on the employment side are closed, and the school is frequently modifying the curriculum on the basis of employer and student needs. Programs are designed specifically to develop marketable job skills, nonacademic as well as academic. For example, after learning that potential employers are just as concerned about personal responsibility and general working skills as they are about the specific job training a student receives, this institution adopted a mandatory attendance policy and started to provide attendance reports along with standard grades on the transcript. Students can be kicked out of the program for poor attendance.

Improvements in convenience and student service appear to be an important way for R institutions to improve their reputations and increase the number of students served. This suggests that traditional institutions underestimate the relative importance of the nonprice costs of obtaining higher education. One private R institution we visited operates many small branch locations and emphasizes convenient course scheduling options and student services. This institution is extremely attractive to students who are frustrated by the lack of options provided by public colleges and universities, which have been buffered from many of the pressures felt by private institutions because they posses a distinct price advantage. However, even the public R institutions we visited were devoting enormous effort toward improving student services.

Although the specific goals of public and private, nonprofit and private, for-profit R institutions differ slightly, the general focus of all of them is to produce value added for the student and to demonstrate that value. Because they compete with one another on the basis of this value added that is generated for the student, successful R institutions tend to be outward looking—continuously monitoring the needs of students, changing their programs in order to respond to changes in customer demands or economic conditions, and identifying and satisfying the needs of new groups of customers.

For P and PS institutions the market for students is a vehicle for investment in prestige as well as for revenue generation. Like R institutions, P and PS schools view students as a source of revenue and develop admission and pricing strategies in order to generate as much revenue as they can. At the same time, P and PS institutions need to attract students with particular qualities in order to maintain or increase their prestige. In certain instances, an institution may place more value on a student's potential contribution to prestige than it does on that student's direct contribution to revenues. Our site visits suggest that it is becoming increasingly difficult for institutions to balance these two objectives.

Research suggests that students do indeed benefit from attending a prestigious school; however, the sources of that benefit are unclear.[3] Many argue that the benefits are largely derived from the screening function: the mere fact that a student graduates from a prestigious institution sends a signal to the world about that student's quality and motivation. Others argue that these institutions actually do provide students with important benefits—both direct educational benefits as well as important networking benefits. Reality is probably somewhere in between.

The mechanism through which institutions benefit from prestige in the market for students is equally unclear. There is some indication that faculty benefit from prestige in the student market by getting students who are smarter, more motivated, and hence easier and more interesting to teach. Research suggests that the prestige derived from national program rankings has an important influence on the college attendance decisions of high-income, high-performing students (McDonough et al. 1997). However, institutions do not appear to benefit from markedly higher tuition than that of less prestigious institutions. The president of one P undergraduate-focused institution stressed that the most prestigious institutions are underpriced and could easily charge 20 percent more. As we discuss later, the primary financial benefit from prestige in the student market may be derived from increased private giving.

Institutions build prestige in the market for students by bringing in students with high test scores and grades, by lowering acceptance rates, and by improving admissions yield rates. The importance of these elements is heavily reinforced by the growing prominence of college ranking systems that incorporate these very elements. The pursuit of prestige thus drives institutions to improve their public images and the perceived desirability of their institutions. However, unlike R institutions, which try to increase customer awareness in order to serve more customers, most P and PS institutions do not intend to serve more customers: they increase applications so that they can reject a higher proportion of them and bring in higher-quality students.

Among both public and private nonprofit institutions, the drive for prestige has led to a significant amount of marketing activity on the part of P and PS institutions—admissions and public relations are a big business. Public schools are less concerned with such marketing, but even they are involved in it—particularly the public institutions in states with stagnant populations. Institutions use a variety of mechanisms to generate interest among potential students, such as direct mail, contact with high schools, and sending videos to individuals or high schools. Successful sports teams also have an important impact on an institution's visibility and hence the number of applications (Dodd 1997). Institutions that are trying to improve prestige in the student market also work to improve the aesthetic features of their campuses or to provide students with more consumption benefits in the form of smaller classes, computer (or athletic or music) facilities, nicer living spaces, or campus social events. At one P institution, the board of trustees asked administrators to list all the things that discourage students from attending the institution. They then allocated more than ten million dollars for such "upfront investment" as renovating the student union, installing fiber optics in the student buildings and Greek houses, and improving student services. Several institutions mentioned a need to invest resources in improving career services for students.

Another way that colleges and universities can potentially increase the number of applications, improve quality, and increase yield is by expanding their scope in a way that expands their potential customer base, for instance, a regionally focused institution begins recruiting nationally; an all-male college begins admitting women. Prestige can be defined in the context of a specific market segment, and an institution can benefit from such prestige. The most prestigious women's colleges or the most prestigious art colleges are widely viewed as successful. However, a strategy based on prestige that stems from a narrow segment of the student market is risky—if the market segment shrinks, even the most prestigious institution in that niche may have trouble maintaining its P resource allocation strategy.

We observed several P and PS institutions that had chosen to build and maintain prestige in their specific regional market—some had been very successful. However, in several states, the most prestigious, regional, private schools were facing serious competition for students from the prestigious public institution in the state. We also observed institutions that were trying to increase their geographic scope while maintaining prestige. This was particularly important for schools in the Midwest, where the number of college-age students was stable or declining. Similarly, most of the religious-oriented P and PS institutions were broadening their scope, each trying to make the institution attractive to students outside of the particular denomination with which it is affiliated.

Institutions that are trying to build or maintain prestige at a national and general level have a strong incentive to become more and more inclusive—broadening the social, demographic, racial, and gender characteristics of students who might find the institution attractive, thereby increasing the number of "high-quality" students from which they can draw. For example, most prestigious institutions have dropped any direct religious, racial, or gender restrictions on admission.

Many P and PS institutions are pulled in opposite directions by the desire to attract the best students in order to improve prestige and the desire to maximize tuition revenue. As we noted at the start of this chapter, tuition revenue does not come only from the students. In fact, it is rare for students to pay the full, posted "sticker" price for attendance. A large fraction of students receive financial aid in the form of grants and scholarships, work study, or subsidized or unsubsidized loans—from federal, state, and private sources external to the institution—which partially offsets the posted tuition/fees payable. For example, while the average annual cost of an independent college (including room and board) was more than $18,000 in 1995, the average student paid about half that. At P and PS colleges and universities, as many as 70 percent of the students receive some institutional aid, and the average "tuition discount" (the difference between the sticker price and the average tuition revenue an institution actually receives) can be as high as 60 percent. Although tuition discounting is most significant at private institutions, many public institutions also offer tuition discounts. For example, the average tuition discount is 39 percent at the University of Virginia and 33 percent at the University of Michigan (*U.S. News & World Report* 1996b).

Traditionally, tuition discounting has been based on financial need—institutions effectively lower the tuition so that it equals the amount the student can afford to pay after all other sources of grants and loan opportunities are taken into account. To a greater and greater extent, the conflict between the need for tuition and the student's contribution to an institution's prestige through high test scores and grades is being reflected in financial aid policy. It is becoming more and more difficult for institutions to maintain the basic tenets of need-based financial aid. The increasing tendency on the part of institutions to use financial aid "strategically" has received a good deal of attention in recent years (Stecklow 1996). If there are two students with the same financial need, a school will offer more aid to the student who is more attractive to the institution and who is more likely to be drawn away by another institution. This process blurs the line between need-based aid and financial aid and leads the industry down the path of price competition.

One PS institution had a long-standing practice of offering merit-based awards to international students in order to improve the quality of the student body. This strategy contributed to a financial crisis at the institution, and one administrator stressed that one of his greatest challenges was convincing other administrators at the institution that you have to bring in some students who can actually pay the tuition. Interestingly, even a public P institution mentioned that it is putting pressure on the state to allow it to offer more attractive financial aid awards to out-of-state students, noting that public institutions in other states were doing that and drawing students away from them.

P and PS institutions must compete for talented students. Institutions interested in increasing the level of prestige must spend resources to provide additional benefits to students or discount tuition to attract students away from more prestigious institutions. In general, an institution's expenditures on these items are inversely related to their level of current prestige—that is, less prestigious institutions have to spend more to convince a student to attend. As competition increases, institutions generally have to spend more on investments in prestige because of the need to "keep up with the Joneses." To the extent that these investments appear as costs of operation for the nonprofit institutions, competition has the effect of increasing the costs of operation for P and PS institutions.

A P or PS resource allocation strategy in the market for students requires that institutions have sources of revenue besides tuition. For prestigious institutions, this other source is private giving or endowment revenue. For tuition dependent schools, a P or PS strategy becomes more complicated. As these institutions spend more to attract bright students, they also have to be sure to attract students who are paying the full tuition. Indeed, in the context of our site visits, we observed a strong and increasing tendency to link the amount of the tuition discount with merit and relaxed admission standards for those who are able to pay the full price. This two-tiered admission policy is more overt at PS institutions, but is even creeping into P institutions. At one PS university that offered generous scholarships to attract talented students, an administrator noted that it was in the unfortunate position of having to "take someone dumb and rich in order to get someone poor and smart."

A more covert use of a two-tiered admission strategy is reflected in early admission programs. These programs provide students with an opportunity to learn whether they have been accepted at an institution of their choice early—before the application deadline at most institutions. A student may apply to only one institution under this early decision program and is normally obliged to attend if accepted.[4]

This program contributes to institutional prestige by increasing yield rates. It also helps the institutions financially in two ways: first, because the program is more likely to appeal to full-pay students, institutions can increase the number of full-pay students by accepting more students early; second, because students are obliged to attend the institution, the school does not have to offer financial aid above the level of "need" to ensure that the student will not decide to attend another institution. There has been a dramatic increase over the past few years in the use of early decision programs among prestigious colleges and universities (Morganthau and Nayyar 1996a Weiss 1997b).

As costs at the private schools increase (in part, due to competition in the market for prestige), more and more bright students determine that the signaling value and additional consumption provided by private institutions is not worth the additional cost and decide to attend the public institutions. This increases the prestige of public institutions, further diminishing the differential between the private and public institutions and leading more students to opt for the public institutions. In several of the states we visited, all but the most elite P and PS schools said that their main competition for students were state public P universities. Several private institutions (in different states) even claimed that the average family income of students at their institutions was lower than that of students at the P public institutions. Higher-income students who are admitted to the public institution are not eligible for financial aid at the private institutions and cannot justify the large additional expense of the private institutions.[5]

Public P research institutions face less pressure in the competition for talented students because the relatively lower tuition generates student demand for enrollment. As long as the differences in the quality of student services is not egregiously worse at the public institutions, many students are willing to sacrifice some service for a much lower-priced education. Many public universities, such as the University of Maryland and the University of Michigan, have compromised by creating small, high-quality, selective "honors colleges" within the larger institution. These units provide a higher level of service and perhaps a higher-quality education to the brightest students who might be tempted to go elsewhere (Applebome 1996). As a result, these institutions can be increasingly selective while devoting fewer resources toward actually satisfying student demands. Although many public schools are protected from declining enrollments by the price differential between the publics and privates, this advantage cannot always make up for fundamental changes in the underlying demographics. One P public institution in a midwestern state that is experiencing a decline in the college age population is investing resources and attention to improving student services.

It is important to stress that institutions do not build prestige in the student market by being innovative or by identifying and meeting new types of student demands. Rather, they build prestige by essentially mimicking the institutions that already have prestige. As a result, prestige-based and prestige-seeking behavior tends to limit innovation. Competition in the student market induces P and PS institutions to become more and more selective. It does not appear to encourage institutions to expand their course offerings or to adopt pedagogical innovations. The drive on the part of institutions to provide a better and better signal of student quality generates an interesting dynamic where the best students are concentrated to a greater and greater extent in the most elite institutions (see Cook and Frank 1993 for formal evidence on this point).

Hybrid institutions often adopt different resource allocation strategies for different segments of the market for students. At the private hybrid institution mentioned earlier, the undergraduate college and the law school were clearly PS entities, whereas the graduate programs were R entities. Administrators made a strong distinction between the undergraduate and law students, who were drawn to the institution because of the quality of and access to faculty, and the other graduate students, who seek a convenient education. The undergraduate and law programs are traditional, full-time residential programs offered at the extremely beautiful but remote main campus; the graduate programs are offered at a variety of locations throughout the metropolitan area, employ mainly adjunct or part-time faculty, and are frequently changed or modified to respond to the demands of students. Another private school we visited employed a PS strategy for its traditional, liberal arts undergraduate education and an aggressive R strategy for its law school, which was located away from the main campus.

Research Funding

Over the past several decades, research advances have contributed to national security, improved the quality of health care and education, promoted economic growth, and improved understanding of the environment. U.S. research universities have made significant contributions to these accomplishments. Although it is difficult to measure the impact of research on society, the superiority of U.S. research universities is widely acknowledged (see, e.g., Office of Technology Assessment 1991). Funding for research and development provides a significant source of revenue to the higher education industry, over $17 billion in 1994.

Research revenue is generated from a variety of sources and supports a wide array of research and development activities performed for a diverse customer base which includes private profit-making concerns; philanthropic organizations; and federal, state, and local governments. Figure 4.4 indicates that federal research funding is dominant, making up 73 percent of the total. State governments provide 9 percent of the funding and industry 8 percent, with founda-

Figure 4.4
Sponsored Research Funding by Source, 1972 to 1994

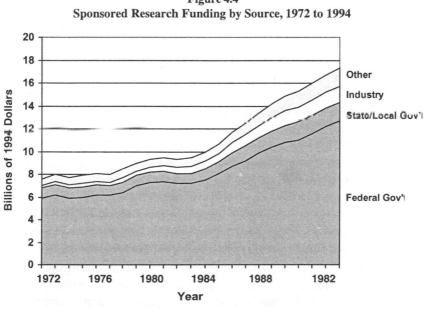

Source: National Science Foundation Data reported in CASPAR.

tions and other organizations providing the remaining 10 percent.[6] Institutions of higher education compete with one another for these resources. They also compete with federal laboratories, government agencies, profit-making firms, and nonprofit organizations. In addition, because of the prestige-generating potential for sponsored research, institutions provide substantial funds under their control (not shown in Figure 4.4). While all such funds are not uniformly reported, the reported amount totaled $3.8 billion in 1994.

Funding for "research and development" supports a range of activities. At one end of the spectrum is applied development and commercialization: activities that generate observable results of known value to an identifiable customer in a relatively short amount of time. For example, a pharmaceutical company might contract with a university hospital to conduct clinical trials of a new drug. At the other end of the spectrum are "basic" research activities that are highly speculative and the benefits of which are difficult to evaluate, document, and appropriate (Office of Technology Assessment 1991). These often have the features of a public good. Although the research is likely to benefit society as a whole, no single individual has an incentive to pay for it. As a result, these activities are normally funded through research grants from the federal government, although private entities and state governments also support such research. Outcomes of this type of research activity are difficult to measure objectively, at least in the short run. As a result, customers of this type of research must rely on a number of indirect evaluation criteria, one of which is the research prestige of the institution.

In the research realm, prestige has its origins at the departmental rather than institutional level. One of the most important measures of prestige is the National Research Council (NRC) rankings. The NRC periodically ranks departments within schools by discipline on the basis of a number of factors, including a poll of professors regarding the prestige of other schools.

Prestige in the research market is based on disciplinary boundaries. Individual departments or programs within an institution are compared with similar programs at other institutions. To the extent that an institution develops prestige in the research market, that prestige is based on the number of prestigious departments or on programs it has or the proportion of its programs that are prestigious. The prestige of individual departments can boost the prestige of other, related departments within the institution. Finally, the prestige of individual departments generates prestige for the institution as a whole, as people begin to associate high-quality research in a specialized field with quality research more generally. We call this the "halo effect" of research prestige. An extreme example is reflected in one study of prestige (Arenson 1997). This study declared that California Institute of Technology had one of the nation's top 25 psychology departments when Cal Tech did not, in fact, have a psychology department at all! Institutions often report the number of departments in the top 5 (or 10 or 20) of the NRC rankings. Institutions will also point to aggregate numbers of prestigious awards won by faculty (such as Nobel prizes or MacArthur awards).

Interesting is that another important measure of prestige at both the department and institutional level is the amount of federal research funding. It has been institutionalized in the Carnegie Classification system for institutions of higher education, which distinguishes among research institutions on the basis of the total amount of federal research funding brought into the institution. One institution we visited was extremely proud of the fact that it had recently achieved the status of a Carnegie Research University II institution, the second highest Carnegie classification in terms of federal research funding. The institution was continuing to strive to increase its federally sponsored research funding in order to achieve the highest category, Carnegie Research University I. Institutions themselves cite the level of federal research funding as a measure of an institution's quality, and even state governments are using it as a measure of the performance of research universities (Bottrill and Borden 1994; Ruppert 1994). The origin of this attribution of prestige to institutions that receive federal research funding is unclear. It might stem in part from the merit-based, competitive review process that is used to allocate much of the federal funding.

In the market for students, we examined the differences between institutions that followed R vs. those that followed, PS or P resource allocation strategies. In the market for research funding, we must also examine whether the institution even participates in the market. A research emphasis is a strategic option for institutions, but it is by no means required. Although the market for research funding is substantial, only relatively few institutions of higher education do in fact participate in the market. In 1994, about 450 institutions reported receiving federal funds for research; this leaves over 3,000 institutions in the industry that do not compete for research funding. We witnessed R, PS, and P institutions that had chosen not to pursue research activities. These institutions were of various types (public and private control, broad and narrow scope) and reflected a variety of goals. These institutions did not specifically explain why they were not pursing research—their statements of goals generally emphasized education and service to the community.

Upfront, fixed costs appear to be an important factor influencing institutions' participation in the market for research, particularly scientific research. Institutions need to make three basic types of investments in order to support research activities. First, they need to invest in research facilities, especially laboratories, libraries, computer facilities, and management. Second, they must attract research-oriented faculty to the institution. Finally, they need to provide graduate education through the Ph.D. degree. The amount of investment required to start a research program clearly varies by discipline. At several institutions, we heard about the start-up expenses (upwards of $250,000) involved in hiring and equipping a single good scholar in the biological sciences. In the case of a tenured faculty member, these upfront costs are dwarfed by the long-term commitment that the school must make.

In many cases, institutions must make a substantial investment in human and physical resources before they can compete for research funding. In deciding whether to engage in research activities, most institutions face a "chicken and egg" problem. Institutions cannot attract funding before they have the resources to provide the research services, but it is expensive to acquire those resources. They must invest the money to build such facilities long before any funding to support the research activity appears. This is a risky investment, which many schools are not willing to make.

R institutions feel two pressures against building a research emphasis. First, they often lack the discretionary resources needed to make the investment in research infrastructure. Second, they recognize that a focus on research might diminish their ability to serve the needs of students (the main customers) and threaten short-run revenue generating ability.

One public, comprehensive R institution we visited was contemplating an increased emphasis on research through the creation of an industrial park/laboratory partnership that would allow it to provide contract research for local business. Although the institution could not expect the state to put up the capital investment needed to build a research infrastructure, it was hoping to generate private donations for the creation of this industrial park. Administrators at two for-profit R schools stressed that their education process was "efficient" precisely because faculty were focused on teaching and not research. Similar considerations about the availability of investment resources and the impact of investment in research on current activities influences the decisions of institutions that have or are seeking prestige in the market for student enrollments. For P or PS institutions, investment in research might cause the institution to sacrifice prestige in its current markets.

The halo effect of research prestige provides an incentive for institutions to expand their research activities into new areas. There appears to be pressure for research universities to be comprehensive—to build strong research programs in more and more fields of study. This incentive to expand the scope of the institution's research activities is countered by the cost involved. It is expensive to maintain a broad infrastructure, and many prestigious research institutions are publicly acknowledging that they cannot afford to maintain a high level of prestige in every field and are thinking about focusing resources in particular areas (Kotch 1997; Fink and Saulnier, 1997). Indeed, some of the most successful universities are those that have specialized their research. As in the student market, a focused strategy can have significant risks in addition to rewards. Specialized institutions need to expand selectively or even shift their emphasis bit by bit in response to changes in funding opportunities. One focused research institution we visited is constantly striving to maintain flexibility by continuing with core research while allocating additional funds for seed projects in order to remain "on the cutting edge." One P research institution that focused mainly on research in the humanities, social sciences, and basic (not applied) physical and life sciences was struggling to respond to dramatic cuts in research funding in the fields in which it has high prestige.

PS institutions are trying to build prestige in the research market. They expressed goals such as "developing international prominence in key programs of graduate study and research." Since these schools do not currently have a high level of prestige, they are at a disadvantage when competing for federal research funding. Recognizing that they cannot afford to invest in all fields of research simultaneously, they typically target their investment in prestige in specific areas. The president of one public, PS research university described how they have to adopt creative hiring strategies. They know they can not attract someone who is an established luminary in a hot field, so instead they try to predict what the "hot areas of the future" will be and hire good junior people in those areas, letting them grow with the university. In this way the institution might be able to build a better reputation for research, although a large number of such hires may not work out as anticipated.

Federal research funding is an important component of prestige in the research market, and institutions must compete for this funding. Colleges and universities compete for federal research dollars on the basis of their current level of prestige as well as cost. An institution's prestige in the research market is derived from current levels of research funding and the reputations of individual faculty members. An institution's current level of research funding also plays an important role in its ability to attract additional funding. Competition therefore has a "rich get richer" property, although competition is tempered by the general political tendency of government to distribute resources widely.

Although nearly all research institutions were following P or PS resource allocation strategies, we did observe a few R institutions that were engaging in research activities. These were public universities with broad scope. Although they clearly took the research activities seriously, in stating their goals, they stressed that research must serve the needs of the local community. The president of one such R research university noted that the goals of his institution reflected a "variation on the trinity." The traditional research, teaching, and public service goals have been imbued with a regional imperative: research is done for economic growth in the region, teaching provides students with immediate job prospects, and public service takes the form of broad access to the higher education system. Another R institution interviewee spoke of the need for complete integration between the university and the local community and for contribution to the economic development of the state through research. Although these institutions do receive federal research funding, the research activities are also related to specific local or regional needs and are directed toward results that benefit identifiable customers (for example, either the needs of local businesses or clinical research in the health area). In spite of the engagement in research, faculty and administrators at these institutions stressed the fact that teaching was valued as least as much as research and complained about the teaching preparation of new Ph.D.s coming out of the prestigious research universities.

Public Fiscal Support

The U.S. higher education industry includes both privately and publicly controlled entities providing a wide array of educational outputs. In spite of these differences, most institutions of higher education receive some revenue from government sources.[7] From the perspective of institutions, there are three distinct types of governmental customers: federal, state, and local. Together, governments provided over $70 billion to institutions of higher education in 1993-94, accounting for 41 percent of the total revenue of the sector, as shown in Table 4.2. The federal government allocated approximately $23.7 billion, or 14 percent of total industry revenue, to institutions of higher education.[8] State governments allocated nearly $42 billion and local governments nearly $5 billion to institutions of higher education, comprising 25 percent and 3 percent respectively, of total industry revenue

The amounts in Table 4.2 reflect the total government spending on higher education; the market for public fiscal support is only one part of that total spending. Much of the public spending on higher education is allocated to institutions through the market for students of the market for research funding. The remaining money is appropriated to schools directly. These appropriations constitute the mar-

Table 4.2
Government Spending on Higher Education
(billions of 1994 dollars)

	Private	Public	Total
Federal	7.7	16.0	23.7
State	1.5	40.2	41.8
Local	.5	4.5	5.0
Total	9.7	60.7	70.5

Table 4.3
Public Fiscal Support of Higher Education
(billions of 1994 dollars)

	Private	Public	Total
Federal	0.2	1.8	2.0
State	0.4	37.2	37.6
Local	0	4.0	4.0
Total	0.6	43.0	43.6

ket for public fiscal support. Federal, state, and local governments differ with respect to the way they choose to allocate resources to the higher education sector. Whereas 84 percent of federal funding flows through the market for research funding in the form of contracts and grants and the market for students in the form of scholarships, state and local governments generally support institutions directly through appropriations while the federal government supports the activities of the institution not the institution directly. Ninety percent of state and 80 percent of local support is allocated through appropriations. Table 4.3 shows the amounts of public fiscal support. With the exception of the appropriations of a few states (in particular, Pennsylvania, New York, New Jersey, and Illinois), most state and nearly all local appropriations are reserved for public institutions.

Government support for higher education has an impact on the activities of individual institutions and on the industry as a whole. When we look at total government spending on higher education, we find that on average public institutions receive 56 percent and private institutions 17 percent of their total revenue from government sources. In private institutions, federal financing accounts for the largest component of government support for higher education, followed by state and then local support. For public institutions, the state is the major source of support, followed by the federal and local government.

While these differences are striking, they suggest that both public and private institutions receive a substantial amount of funding with public origins. However, when we look specifically at the market for public fiscal support defined as appropriations from government to colleges and universities, we observe that the primary players in this market are state governments and public institutions. Table 4.4 shows the percentage of revenues derived from public fiscal support for private and public institutions. Only a trace of the revenue of private institutions comes from government appropriations, reflecting the fact that these institutions are not significant participants in the market for public fiscal support. Public schools, on the other hand, receive 34 percent of their revenue from state governments on average, and a small fraction from federal and local government. Two-year public institutions are the most highly dependent on public fiscal support, receiving 39 percent of their revenue from state and 19 percent from local appropriations.

Public fiscal support plays a small role in the revenues of privates, and, not surprisingly, none of those we visited mentioned service to the state or nation as a major goal.[9] More interesting is the fact that, within the set of public institutions, institutions differed significantly with respect to the emphasis they placed on state needs. We found that all public institutions at least acknowledge the interests of the state when describing their institutional goals, each noting some variation of "serving the needs of the public" as one of the major goals for which the institution is striving.

The general goal of serving state needs was manifest in different ways at different institutions. Community colleges asserted a desire to serve the local community by providing access to higher education, training the workforce, and providing cultural events and other services to the community. Schools granting bachelor's, master's, and doctoral degrees mentioned a need to provide state residents with access to a quality education at a low cost or to provide citizens with the opportunity to succeed. Some articulated this goal in terms of raising the economic and educational level of the region or state they serve.

Table 4.4
Public Fiscal Support as a Percent of Total Revenue

	Federal	State	Local
Private	0	0	0
Public (all)	1	34	3
Public—2 year	0	39	19

Despite the apparent consistency across publics in terms of the articulation of the goal of serving state needs, there were distinct differences in the ways this goal was framed and implemented. At R institutions, the objective of serving state or local needs seemed to motivate the activities of the institution. Many were pursuing a favored position vis-à-vis the government, but they were doing so by demonstrating responsiveness to community needs. These institutions attempt to determine the specific nature of community wants and needs, incorporate what they learn into their academic and vocational programs, and monitor whether these needs are met. This strategy is further supported by enrollment-based funding[10] mechanisms that push institutions to identify new demands in order to increase enrollment. For example, one R public institution developed credentialing programs for nurses and was offering these on site at local hospitals. The same institution had developed a special psychology program for police officers. R institutions stated goals such as "offering education with the least disruption to the students' lives" and simply to "provide post-secondary education to the community."

Public P and PS schools were not concerned as much with identifying and meeting the needs of state residents and state leaders as they were with improving their national, regional, or local images by framing what they were doing in such a way that the legislature and the public would credit their service to the state. The fundamental premise appeared to be that the university was doing important things and that their activities would certainly benefit the state, region, or nation. Their main task was thus to convince the government or its citizens of this fact. When asked about the challenges they face, these institutions cited "communicating what we do to the public" and demonstrating the relevance of the institution's research for society. One public PS institution articulated the goals of "achieving international prominence in key programs of graduate study and research" and to "be America's leading partnership university." One public, P research university stressed the challenge of "addressing ourselves to an external environment that expects the same things from us but requires a different language" and stated a need to bring the intellectual strength of the institution to the community. This institution was trying to fit its current activities into the perceived obligation.

Public two-year colleges, which are dependent largely on state and local funding, are extremely responsive to community needs. All the community colleges we visited, even one we classified as a P institution, were concerned about meeting the needs of the local government. The activity mix of the institutions depended on their locations. For example, one community college was extremely isolated, located in the middle of several small communities that it serves. This school focuses on providing education and training to students. Another community college, located in an affluent metropolitan area, provides an entire array of services to the community, including adult education/enrichment courses, ESL courses, as well as the sponsoring of cultural and social events. Administrators at one college mentioned "figuring out what societal needs we are supposed to be filling" as one of the major challenges facing them. Because support is tied to the local community, these institutions normally have to be sensitive to the impact they have on their neighborhoods, and have to work harder than other schools to be "good neighbors."

Several institutions mentioned public relations as an important challenge. Whereas most state taxpayers cannot witness the impact of each state university firsthand, local taxpayers are more likely to have direct contact with their local community college. Although all public two-year institutions highlighted the importance of reputation, we did observe one that also exhibited features of a prestige-based resource allocation strategy. This institution had developed prestige in its local/regional market, boasting a high transfer rate to well-known, four-year institutions in the area. This institution attracts students from throughout the metropolitan area in which it is located and a sizable number of foreign students. Although the relative emphasis of prestige-building versus reputation-building is different from that witnessed in a P research institution, P community colleges do appear to reap gains from their prestige in terms of local community support, ability to pay professors higher salaries, etc.

Several of the public institutions we visited were facing increased demands for accountability from the state governments. Such demands influence institutional strategies in a complicated way. On the most simplistic level, they threaten the success of P resource allocation strategies and support R strategies. Public R institutions are by definition oriented toward identifying and serving the needs of their constituents and performance-based funding mechanisms that reward them for meeting state objectives. For these schools, the biggest challenge is how they can measure and demonstrate the various ways in which they serve state needs, and many performance-based funding mechanisms provide a system for doing that. For P and PS institutions however, these demands are often inconsistent with investment in prestige because they must devote discretionary resources toward meeting specific government demands that are often unrelated to prestige. Several of the P and PS institutions we visited are responding with attempts to "educate" the public as to what they really do, and to convince the legislature of the "special" nature of what they do, stressing that they serve "different" state needs which are not easily quantifiable and that they cannot be expected to meet the same targets as R institutions.

Because of their prestige and the resources they bring into the state, public P institutions (which are almost always research universities) often have a good deal of bargaining power vis-à-vis the state. This power provides them with the opportunity to negotiate different funding arrangements with the state, even in the face of strong accountability demands. In many states where performance indicator systems are being developed or other sorts of mandates are being instituted, the P institutions have been successful in inducing the states to modify the criteria to account for their special role in the state (Ruppert 1994). PS institutions have the most to lose as states increase demands for accountability. They would like to emulate the strong bargaining power that P institutions have with the state. One PS institution explicitly mentioned that they receive per student funding that is below the state average and that they need to improve their status in order to receive a bigger piece of the state higher education budget. However, PSs do not currently have the cachet, and hence the bargaining power, of the P institutions and are therefore under pressure to respond to existing state demands. As a result, they are torn between devoting resources to meet the demands of the public (and thus maintaining their reputation) and devoting resources toward activities to help them build prestige.

Only public institutions can cash in on prestige in the market for public fiscal support, and the rewards of prestige available through this market will depend on the level of and anticipated growth in state spending on higher education. In states where resources devoted to the higher education sector and the college-age population are expected to grow, institutions may find that it is worthwhile to invest in prestige in order to increase stature within the state and improve institutional autonomy. In states with declining college-age populations, or where state funding for higher education is not expected to grow, this resource allocation strategy is more risky. The result of this may be a geographical shift in the amount of prestige among public institutions from the Rust Belt, where population growth is stagnant, to the Sun Belt, where there is strong population growth.

Perhaps in response to accountability demands placed on them by the state, some P public institutions are pushing to diversify their revenue base in order to reduce their dependence on the state, although it is not clear whether these are empty threats intended to further increase the institutions bargaining power vis-à-vis the state or actions being seriously considered.

Private Giving

Private giving to institutions of higher education takes many forms and comes from a variety of sources. It includes restricted and unrestricted gifts and grants, cash payments returned as contributions from salaried staff, and insurance premiums paid by donors. Institutions of higher education received an estimated $12.4 billion in voluntary support in 1994 and an additional $3.7 billion from endowment income, accounting for 7.3 percent and 2.2 percent respectively of the sector's total revenue. As Table 4.5 illustrates, most private giving to higher education takes the form of alumni donations, followed by contributions from nonalumni individuals, foundations, and corporations. Religious organizations provide a small fraction of total voluntary support to higher education.

Endowment earnings, while a small fraction of the sector's revenue, are an extremely important revenue source for a small group of institutions. Endowment income is extremely concentrated, with the top 10 institutions accounting for almost 30 percent of all endowment income.[11] The top 50 institutions account for 55 percent of the industry total and the top 100 for 69 percent of the total. As expected, endowment income is concentrated in private institutions, which receive 82 percent of the total endowment income. On average, private institutions receive 4.7 percent of their total revenue from endowment income, as opposed to 0.6 percent for public institutions.

Table 4.5
Estimated Voluntary Support of Higher Education,
by Source and Purpose, 1994

	Amount (millions of dollars)	Percentage of Total
Total Voluntary Support	12,350	(100)
Sources		
Alumni	3,410	(28)
Nonalumni individuals	2,800	(23)
Corporations	2,510	(20)
Foundations	2,540	(21)
Religious organizations	240	(2)
Other	850	(7)
Purposes		
Current operations	6,710	(54)
Capital purposes	5,640	(46)

Source: Voluntary Support of Education 1995.
Note: Figures in parentheses are percentages of total and may not sum to 100 percent due to rounding.

The market for private giving is growing; the total value of private giving to higher education has been increasing over time. This increase is due more to private giving for current operations than to giving for buildings and endowment, as shown in Figure 4.5. Along with this growth has come increased attention on the part of colleges and universities to this market.

The market for private giving is a more important source of revenue for private than for public schools. Figure 4.6 reveals that private donations account for over 20 percent of the revenues of private liberal arts colleges and over 15 percent of total revenues for private research universities. For other privates the fraction is smaller but still significant.

With the exception of the for-profit institutions, all the schools we visited were interested in increasing revenue derived from private giving. Although some had clearly made progress toward that goal, others were struggling with implementation of fundraising strategies. As in many other markets, we noticed a significant difference between

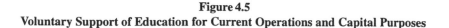

Figure 4.5
Voluntary Support of Education for Current Operations and Capital Purposes

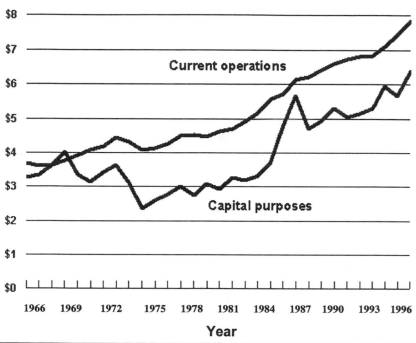

Source: Voluntary Support of Education 1996.

P, PS, and R institutions with respect to their strategic behavior in the market for private giving. R institutions were much more likely to focus on market-based relationships with the private sector, such as developing business partnerships or providing contract teaching services, whereas PS and P institutions emphasized the more altruistic relationships with the private sector. We also observed a distinction between publics and privates: whereas the latter have recognized the importance of private giving for some time, the former were only beginning to exploit this source of revenue.[12]

One of the surprising observations from our visits was the growing realization of the importance of private sector support by public colleges and universities. Presidents and administrators of these schools articulated a need to increase private support either to compensate for declines in state funding for their institutions or for projected declines in enrollment. In several states, the new focus on

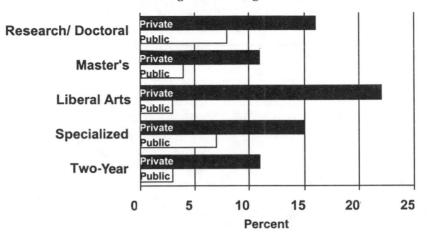

Figure 4.6
Private Giving as a Percentage of Revenue

fundraising has also been influenced by changes in state policy. Heretofore, many states and/or state higher education systems forbade public institutions from soliciting private sector donations. This attitude appears to be changing; the president of one state institution we visited noted that the state now requires the institution to generate 10 percent of its revenue from private donations. Although many of the schools we visited were only beginning to develop and implement strategies for actually increasing such support, many appeared confident that they would be able to translate their visions into reality. Presidents were aware that fundraising was now a more important part of their jobs than it had been in the past. One president of a broad public university noted that when he first assumed the post seven years earlier fundraising was not even included in his job description but that he now spends a significant amount of time fundraising.

The public institutions rely on private giving to fund at least part of the construction of new facilities. Administrators in all the states we visited were acutely aware of the fact that the state either would not or could not provide for the construction of new facilities. Such capital constraints were especially important for institutions with plans to grow. These schools felt the need to raise private support even more strongly. The need for private funding for construction purposes appears to be widespread. In one state, this is encouraged through an explicit state policy whereby the state matches private donations to universities for construction purposes.

Whereas public institutions stressed the need for private donations for facilities, construction, privates seemed more concerned
about raising money to build their endowment. Because the endowment has the potential to provide a steady stream of income to support the activities of the institution, increasing it is considered to be
the primary alternative to raising tuition. The presidents of several P
and PS privates we visited, particularly those that operate in a regional or local market, expressed a great deal of concern over what
they view as new competition for private donations from public
schools. One president remarked that it did not seem appropriate for
the publics to ask local business and private individuals for donations when they and all other state residents were already "donat-
ing" to the institution through taxes.

The reasons for such concern are clear. In a sense, the market for
private giving is to private institutions what the market for public
fiscal support is to public institutions: a source of flexible revenue
that rewards reputation and prestige.

Fundraising appears to be a key element of the strategy of PS
institutions for moving into the P category and for Ps to remain in
that position. All nonprofit institutions we visited were trying to increase private giving because other sources of revenue (federal research money, state appropriations, or tuition) were either stable or
declining. The relationship between the market for private giving
and other key revenue markets is particularly vivid in primarily undergraduate P institutions, which draw a significant proportion of
their revenue from tuition. At one P liberal arts college in the Midwest, increasing the endowment was articulated to be a critical
element of the institution's strategy. This school is struggling to improve the quality of the student body in the face of rising tuition and
declines in its traditional in-state population base. Administrators want
to avoid the temptation of "dipping deeper in the applicant pool" in
order to fill their classes. Their current plan is to makeup front investments in prestige by offering potential students attractive financial aid packages and improving the attractiveness of the campus.
The board had given the president permission to take larger payouts
from the endowment over the short term to get things started but
stressed that over the long term a larger endowment would be required to sustain such a strategy. Administrators freely acknowledged
that the success of this strategy hinged on their ability to stage successful capital campaigns.

The market for private giving is one in which prestigious institutions are able to reap the rewards of that prestige, for it is prestige (generated through the market for students or the market for research funding) that tends to build donor trust and attract private giving. PS institutions also look to capital campaigns to provide them with the investment capital they need to move into the P category, but they have to work much harder to develop such private support. An administrator of one public PS research university even acknowledged that her institution was not sophisticated enough to attract major private donations. We found that, in general, PS institutions have to be more entrepreneurial in generating the private giving. One hybrid institution we visited had been using surpluses from "market oriented" graduate programs to subsidize its undergraduate program in order to build its prestige. Having achieved a certain level of prestige, this university is now focusing on capital campaigns to grow the endowment. Revenue from endowment will then be used to support the prestige-building activities within the undergraduate program, eliminating the need for cross-subsidies and improving the competitiveness of the reputation-based programs.

Fundraising does not appear to be such an important strategy among the R institutions we visited. While they are certainly interested in attracting gifts and grants, they do not depend on them so that gifts and grants are in some sense treated as windfall revenue. For example, one R liberal arts college had received a $750,000 grant to support undergraduate education in biology. This institution does have an endowment but uses all the income generated toward student scholarships. Another R research university does solicit private donations for the construction of new buildings, thus linking specific projects—but not the overall institutional strategy— to fundraising success. R institutions appear to be much more focused on developing partnerships with businesses or expanding their market-type interactions with the private sector and generating flexible revenue for the institutions in that way.

Institutions also turn to private giving to bail them out of financial crises. It is frequently noted that, whereas it is commonplace for firms to go out of business in the private sector (and for new businesses to be created), there is relatively little entry and exit in the higher education industry. Indeed, only 346 institutions of higher education (312 privates) closed between 1969-70 and 1992-93 (National Center for Education Statistics 1995).[13] In the course of our study, we visited an institution that was recently rescued by a private organization after it had completely spent its endowment. If not for the financial bailout, this institution would likely have been forced to close its doors. The president of this university noted that it made sense for the rescuing organization, which was trying to develop a presence in higher education, to buy an existing but financially troubled institution rather than try to create its own from scratch. As part of the bailout agreement, the donor organization appoints half of the members of the board of trustees and hence has some input into the choice of administrators. Thus while it does not control the institution, it certainly has some influence over the institution's activities and its direction. This may be an effective strategy because the startup costs of opening a university, attracting students, achieving accreditation, etc., are enormous and form a significant barrier to entry. Reputation and name recognition are important assets even for a troubled school—and are more valuable in some cases than the bricks and mortar of the institution.

With the exception of one research university that has relatively low rates of alumni participation in annual giving programs, interviewees at private institutions did not mention alumni giving as a potential source of *growth* in private giving. Indeed, interviewees at most privates mentioned specific challenges they face in trying to maintain current levels of private giving.[14] Religious support was not a major source of revenue, even for the religiously affiliated institutions. One institution receives a "living endowment" from church donations, which accounted for about 4 percent of their current total revenue. However, this amount is based on church donations, which are allocated to all the universities supported by this denomination. As a result of potential instability in this income stream, this institution was trying to build its own endowment to protect itself in the event of a decline in church support.

Although there are no systematic data on the capital campaigns, these appear to be occurring with greater frequency and with larger goals. Almost every private institution was in the middle of a capital campaign to build the endowment, and most were undertaking such campaigns with increasing frequency. Administrators at one institution even commented that they would be beginning another campaign as soon as they finished the current one. Private giving to higher education allows institutions to build their endowment. This endowment generates revenue, which allows the institutions to provide more services to students, faculty, and staff without increasing tuition.[15]

The market for private giving is one in which schools can reap the benefits of prestige and, to a more limited extent, reputation. Evidence from our site visits suggests that donors want to support institutions that are currently doing a good job, not help bail out institutions that are aimless or are being mismanaged. One university in our sample was about to embark upon a major capital campaign but was waiting to start the campaign until it had developed a clear mission statement for the institution. The president of this institution noted that it's much easier to get people to donate if you give them a reason. Administrators at another PS college noted that the college's recent financial troubles and academic repositioning have left the school somewhat vulnerable because people don't want to give to a school experiencing financial trouble. This administrator also noted that foundations ask colleges for information on student demand (number of applications, student test scores, etc.) when awarding grants. Interviewees at several institutions mentioned the fact that successful sports teams can generate additional private giving, particularly from alumni. However, those at one university stressed that high-profile sports teams can also have a negative impact on private giving. The antics of the coach of a perennially nationally ranked team at this university have a tendency to attract a lot of bad press. While the success of the team has a positive influence on donations, this coach has a negative influence on donations and on the university's image. In general, private giving is a reward of prestige and reputation. Institutions that have discretionary revenue and successfully invest it in one of the prestige generators or in reputation are able to attract additional private donations in order to improve quality further.

Overview of the Four Key Revenue Markets

In this chapter we have tried to make some general observations about the resource allocation strategies pursued by institutions in each of the four key revenue markets and provide some specific behavioral examples from our site visits. The most striking observation is that competition has different implications for R institutions than for it does P and PS institutions in each of these markets. Competition among R institutions is not a "zero-sum game"—i.e., one institution can improve its reputation without harming the reputation of others. Reputation does have a comparative component in the sense that an institution benefits from the fact that its reputation is higher than that of competitors. However, competition among Rs can contribute to the value produced by the industry as a whole, thus increasing the total amount of reputation. For example, competition for students induces R institutions to undertake activities that increase the value students derive from educational services and that expand access to higher education.

Competition among P and PS institutions has different implications. It does not in and of itself increase the total value added generated in these markets, although it does influence the way that value added is distributed between institutions and their customers. The amount of prestige in the industry may vary over time, but this variation has less to do with the P or PS strategies pursued by institutions and more to do with exogenous factors outside of the institutions' control. For example, schools improve their prestige in the research market by increasing the amount of federal research money received. Hence, the amount of prestige available through research necessarily depends on the level of federal funding available, which is heavily influenced by the political and economic environment. Institutions build prestige in the student market by improving the "quality" of the student body and increasing the institutions' admission selectivity. The ability of institutions to do this without diminishing the prestige of other institutions depends in part on the number of "bright" students pursuing higher education. This is influenced by demographic factors, social changes (such as the growth in college attendance by women and minorities), access to student loans, and technology. When there is no change in these other factors, a school may increase its prestige, thereby increasing the value that its students derive from the market signal they receive. But such an increase comes at the expense of the prestige of other P and PS institutions.

Because competition has significant implications for the industry, it is important to point out some of the factors influencing competition. In general, competition is strongest in urban areas and weakest in small towns and rural areas. This pattern is not uncommon in service industries. The cost of providing educational services is likely to be higher in rural areas because the fixed costs cannot be distributed over as large a student population. At the same time, the willingness of people in these areas to pay for the education is likely to be lower because of fewer high-paying job prospects. Distance learning technology is often mentioned as a way to expand access to higher education for people who live in remote areas. However, we found that, to the extent that these methods are being used, they are being used in urban or suburban settings. This may be because the institutions in these areas generally provide sites where student groups can meet for project work or locations where students can watch a course over closed-circuit television. As a result, their cost structures imply that there is a benefit to locating in larger population centers.[16]

Competition is weaker for public institutions than it is for private institutions. Public institutions face less competition than private nonprofit and for-profit institutions because government subsidy is used to reduce the price that is charged to other customers (in particular, students). This government subsidy provides publics with a buffer against competitive forces. Even if a public institution offers less value added to the student than private nonprofit or for-profit institutions, students might still attend the public school because of the lower price. Of course, publics in urban areas often face competition from other public institutions. In one state we visited, one of the major public systems had recently relaxed a long-standing prohibition on advertising, and institutions in the same metropolitan area were starting to compete with one another for students. Public schools in geographically isolated areas face the least competition. Normally, there are no other publics that students can conveniently attend, and the private nonprofit and for-profit institutions, even those that use distance learning technology, have not yet penetrated these remote markets.

In the market for student enrollments, R-focused institutions depend on student enrollments for revenue and therefore focus on meeting student needs in a demonstrable way. They are "outward" looking—focused on monitoring and responding to student demands. R institutions are relatively quick to change their product offerings or organizational structure to respond to the changing needs, leading to heterogeneity among institutions, a diversity of service bundles, and innovation in instructional approaches.

Competition among P and PS institutions for students is strong. These institutions want students not only for the financial resources they bring to the school but also for the contributions they can make to the institution's stock of prestige. Maintaining a P or PS, focused strategy is expensive. It often requires heavy tuition discounting and a high level of expenditures on facilities and student services. In addition, because institutions are ultimately pursuing the same type of student, competition among Ps and PSs tends to promote homogeneity among institutions, at least with respect to the core educational technologies. To the extent that such schools distinguish themselves, it is on the basis of secondary characteristics such as the campus atmosphere.

The decision to participate in the market for research is a choice that only a fraction of institutions make. We noted a potential correlation between the resource allocation strategy of institutions and the decision to pursue research: R strategies are currently rare among institutions with a research emphasis. R institutions that do emphasize research stress the need for a balance between the goals of teaching, research, and service. Federal research funding is an important prestige generator; P and PS institutions seek federal research funding for the contribution it makes to both net revenues and prestige. The prestige value of federal research funding induces these institutions to compete for such funding on the basis of cost. This makes it difficult for such institutions to sustain their infrastructure based on federal research funding alone.

Prestige is costly to build and maintain. Because two of the primary prestige generators are student quality indicators and the level of federal research funding, prestige-seeking and prestige-based behavior often leads institutions to sacrifice some of their revenue generating ability in the market for students and the market for research. The rewards from prestige come from the market for public fiscal support and/or the market for private giving.

Public funding for higher education is influenced by political considerations, and prestige appears to influence those funding decisions. Formula-based funding programs tend to favor public institutions with more prestige: they get more state revenue per student or a larger lump-sum transfer. Recently, state governments have been putting pressure on institutions of higher education to demonstrate the ways their activities benefit the state or locale. These increased demands for accountability on the part of state governments threaten P and PS schools more than R-focused ones because they tend to reward institutions on the basis of customer-focused outcome measures. However, prestigious institutions have used their prestige to negotiate for more flexibility and autonomy in the context of accountability programs than their less prestigious public counterparts have. In the event that they can negotiate such arrangements, the rewards are substantial.

The market for private giving also rewards P and PS institutions. R schools are more likely to develop business partnerships or engage in contract education than to pursue altruistic private giving. Prestige appears to help institutions compete for private donations, and the revenue generated through private donations appears to help institutions increase prestige. For example, private institutions rely on private giving to build endowments. Endowments generate resources that can be used for financial aid to attract high-quality students or to support the research infrastructure. Public schools use private gifts primarily for capital spending, again to build the research infrastructure. Fundraising is particularly important for PS schools, which need capital to move into the P group. Because these institutions do not currently have a high level of prestige, they must work even harder to generate the level of giving they require for investments in prestige.

This chapter focused on the relationships between institutions and customers in the four key revenue markets. In the next chapter, we discuss the motivations for and implications of this behavior at the institutional level. We then bring together the industry-wide and institution-specific perspectives in discussing six in-depth case studies.

Notes

1.   This is an economic model that likens schooling decisions to investments.
2.   For some students, proximity to home was the most important factor influencing their decision. In general, the cost of the institution and the perceived economic payoffs were the most frequently cited reasons for choosing the institution they were attending. The prestige of the institution was also a frequently mentioned element—many students said that they went to the "best" institution they could get into. Others were focused on price and only applied to public institutions in their state of residence.
3.   For example, Brewer and Ehrenberg (1996) and Brewer, Eide, and Ehrenberg (1999) show that there is a significant labor market premium to attending an elite private college as an undergraduate. Eide, Brewer, and Ehrenberg (1998) also show

       that students attending such a school increases the probability of that student's attending an elite graduate school.

4.   Brown and Harvard Universities do not require the student to attend if accepted.

5.   Some evidence (Brewer and Ehrenberg 1996; Brewer, Eide, and Ehrenberg 1999, and Eide, Brewer and Ehrenberg 1998) suggests that the payoff to elite private institutions in the labor market and in providing access to graduate school may be significant enough to offset the additional cost burden of attending these schools.

6.   These fractions exclude research supported by university funds.

7.   There are approximately 250 private institutions that reported receiving no revenue from government sources in the 1994 IPEDS database. Most but not all of these institutions are religious schools.

8.   In addition, the federal government spent $22.9 billion on student loan programs and college work-study programs. Since these funds do not go to institutions of higher education directly and are not reported on an institution-by-institution basis in IPEDS, they are excluded from the calculation.

9.   Many private institutions did mention service as a major goal, however, the community to be served might be a particular religious order, or needy people in the local community or in the world. This is different from the goal of educating or serving the educational needs of people in a defined local or regional area.

10.   Enrollment-based funding is a common mechanism for funding public colleges and universities. State governments establish a funding formula that rewards institutions with more money for each additional student (i.e., the level of funding increases with the level of enrollment).

11.   Figures reported in this paragraph are from caluclations based on IPEDS data. One of the "institutions" is the Office of the President of the University of California, which encompasses the nine University of California campuses.

12.   This supports the analyses of national data on voluntary support detailed in Brewer, Gebs, and Goldman (2001).

13.   Recall that the current (1995) number of colleges and universities is 3,706.

14.   Even if alumni donations become a less crucial element of financial strategy they will also play a role in the institution's reputation through rankings like those of *U.S. News & World Report,* which examines the percentage of living alumni who donated to the institution's annual fund (this counts for 5 percent of the score upon which the overall rankings are based). This may lead institutions to try to wage a broad alumni donation campaign, encouraging alumni to donate even a small amount of money, in order to increase their ranking.

15.   The income generated from Harvard's endowment (nearly $400,000 per student in 1995) allows the school to provide students with services that it would not be able to provide otherwise. It is also likely that the faculty and staff reap benefits from this income through higher salaries and greater perquisites.

16.   The largest private "distance learning" institutions have established sites in urban and suburban areas or on military bases—locations where there are high concentrations of potential students. To the extent that distance learning has been used to serve rural communities and small towns, the service has been provided by public institutions (University of Tennessee, University of Alaska, University of Maine), which may be receiving state money to cover the fixed costs.

5

Relating Financial Health to Institutional Position and Strategy: Six Case Studies

To this point in the book we have laid out the ways in which institutions of higher education appear to us to act in the four key revenue markets of student enrollments, research, public fiscal support, and private giving. We have argued that schools choose a multidimensional strategy consistent with their present position in terms of reputation and prestige. We have illustrated some of the choices that institutions make in each of the four revenue markets and highlighted some differences among the three basic strategic types that are so important that we label institutions on the basis of these strategies. But we have not said very much about the relative importance of each of these four markets for a given institution, why and how an institution decides to act in each market, and what the impact of such decisions might be.

In this chapter we tackle these issues by describing the relationships among institutional position, strategy, and financial health. We define financial health, explain how it relates to an institution's present position and choice of strategy, and use case studies of six schools we visited to illustrate these relationships. Following the case studies, we use some quantitative data on a broader spectrum of institutions to generalize the lessons from the case studies.

The Concept of Financial Health

There is substantial concern about the *financial health* of U.S. colleges and universities but little understanding of the elements of that financial health. We suggest that financial health has a short-run and a long-run aspect in the higher education industry. The short-run element relates to the annual condition of the budget: a financially healthy institution balances revenue and expenditure year by year. This is an intuitive criterion—an institution cannot be financially healthy if it spends more than it takes in; however, balancing the budget in a given year does not in and of itself imply long-run financial health. Over the long run, there must be a consistency between current revenues and expenditures and the institution's overall strategy: in a financially healthy institution, revenue and expenditure patterns must be able to support the institution's strategy on the dimensions of degree level, scope, and strategic type.

For profit-making enterprises, financial health is akin to profitability. Stock markets offer continuous estimates of the financial health of publicly traded firms. There is no natural analog for the nonprofit organization. Although higher education institutions report revenues and expenditures, the difference between the reported revenue and the reported expenditure cannot be characterized as profit. Expenditures include both basic operating costs—competitive market-based salaries for the faculty and administrators and the cost of maintaining and operating the campus and its buildings—and discretionary resource spending, which covers investment (in reputation and prestige), savings, and extra consumption.

As noted in Chapter 2, identifying actual operating costs is difficult. Hidden deficits may arise when the institution fails to provide for its true costs of operation. For example, a school can develop a hidden deficit by failing to maintain its buildings or campus, thereby building a backlog of deferred maintenance. Financially healthy colleges set aside reserves to cover the depreciation of buildings and equipment. When those assets need to be replaced, if the institution has not set aside these reserves, it must take funding from another source, perhaps imperiling an important program. A financially stressed institution may decide not to maintain its salary and support budgets at levels appropriate for its type of personnel. On the other hand, if a school is healthy, it provides for maintenance, depreciation, and competitive salaries. If it is not healthy, it can reduce expenditures on these costs of operation. If the financial difficulty is not severe, these reductions in reported costs may allow it to report a budget in balance. In this case the balanced budget conceals the hidden deficit from underspending on operations.

If discretionary spending were removed from reported budgets and hidden deficits were included, then we would have a measure of the short-run aspect of the financial health of an institution. In practice, this is very difficult to do. Instead, other quantitative and qualitative indicators may provide clues to short-run financial health. Endowment spending is just one indicator of current financial health. Other indicators are discussed in our case studies below.

Revenues, Expenditures, and Resource Allocation

As detailed in Chapter 4, an institution's ability to generate revenue is affected by its strategy as well as by market conditions. An institution's resource allocation strategy influences its stock of reputation and prestige, which in turn affects the revenues that the institution can generate and hence the discretionary resources the institution can allocate toward investment in future stocks of reputation, prestige, and endowment. In general, the greater an institution's reputation, the higher prices it can command in most markets. The greater an institution's prestige, the more likely it is to generate research and private giving revenues (though, as we noted in Chapter 4, higher prestige may not bring higher revenue in the student market).

Other dimensions of strategy also influence expenditures. Generally speaking, a position and strategy that are "higher" in terms of the three summary dimensions (degree offerings, scope, and strategic type) require more expenditure on the part of the institution. Broader scope is associated with more programs and activities at an institution. The greater the number of programs, the more revenue that flows into the institution. But costs increase as well. Each additional program requires resources to operate. Higher degree offerings are also associated with more costs for the institution. Faculty salaries are higher, on average, in doctoral-degree granting institutions than in undergraduate or community colleges. And, as we have discussed earlier, P and PS-focused strategies require major investments to seek and maintain prestige, while R-focused strategies do not require these investments.

After paying basic operating costs out of its revenues, an institution may be left with some discretionary resources, which it divides among investment in reputation, investment in prestige, savings, and extra consumption, in line with its strategy. Before we move into the case studies, we will review briefly the basic decisions in resource allocation.

Consumption takes on very different forms in for-profit and in nonprofit organizations. Some colleges and universities are operated by profit-making corporations. In these schools, consumption takes the form of dividends to shareholders or payments to the parent corporation. But most institutions of higher education are nonprofit, without shareholders. Instead, these schools divide consumption among internal stakeholders: the faculty, administrators, and students. Examples of forms of consumption in nonprofit institutions of higher education are high faculty salaries, low faculty teaching loads, and luxurious buildings. Investments in prestige often generate consumption benefits as well, at least for some insiders: some faculty members derive satisfaction from more selective student admissions, or some students enjoy attending a school with a winning basketball team.

Institutions can also save some of their discretionary resources for the future. Some private giving is targeted to the institution's endowment, meaning that the gift must be saved to provide a stream of income for the future. Savings under the discretion of the school (as opposed to planned savings designated by donors) are termed "quasi-endowment," since these funds function as supplements to the endowment.

Endowment and savings management is an important issue for those institutions fortunate enough to have substantial endowments. Institutions whose endowments do not keep up with those of their competitors must ask students—or other customers—to assume a larger share of the cost of their education than these competitors do. One liberal arts college placed a substantial share of its endowment in risky investments and has not earned the return it could have on its endowment in recent years. Although its endowment has increased, its competitors' endowments have increased faster. Administrators at several institutions expressed concern that institutions have become "addicted" to stock market increases and wonder what institutions will do when the market falls.

Because of its importance, the rate of spending from endowment is a primary indicator of short-run financial health. If the endowment spending rate is greater than the growth rate of the endowment's financial investments (minus the growth rate of costs), then the institution is eroding the value of its endowment (Massy 1990). Such institutions will find that their endowments in the future cannot support the same activities they do in the present. Overspending the endowment for more than a few years can be a risky decision.

No one can know for sure what the exact growth rate of the endowment investments (i.e., the rate of return) will be. Likewise, no one can know the exact rate of growth of costs (i.e., inflation). But over time, analysts observe long-term trends in these rates. Based on these long-term analyses, there is a rough consensus that spending about 5 percent of the endowment value per year will maintain a stable endowment (in terms of purchasing power). Institutions with very strong financial health may set their spending rates below 5 percent and thus increase the purchasing power of their endowment gradually over time. When an institution faces financial pressure because of underlying deficits, the board of trustees often raises the endowment spending rate. Thus, institutions that pay out much more than 5 percent annually are likely to be unhealthy. (For a fuller treatment of the management of endowment, see Massy, 1990.)

Stock of and Investment in Reputation and Prestige

Reputation and prestige are valuable because they improve the institution's ability to generate revenue in the four main revenue markets. Prestige benefits institutions by improving revenue generating ability in the markets for public fiscal support and private giving. Although prestige might also provide institutions with the opportunity to temporarily boost revenue through the market for students and research funding as well, the long-run need to maintain prestige through the prestige generators of student quality or federal research funding deters schools from capitalizing on that ability. Reputation, on the other hand, improves an institution's ability to generate revenue through the markets for students, research, and public fiscal support. Reputation gives institutions a competitive advantage in a particular market, allowing the institution to retain a higher proportion of the value added it generates through its activities.

The value of reputation is influenced by features of the market. When competition is strong, institutions stand to benefit from more reputation (either by attracting more customers or by charging a higher price); conversely, they can lose market share or their ability to charge a higher price if their reputation declines. When institutions do not face a lot of competition, potential gains from improving their reputation are limited. They have less incentive to improve productivity because their revenue generating capability is not being eroded by competition. Gains from improving reputation are also limited if the institution is facing capacity constraints and cannot expand without a significant capital investment. This was the case at one remote R institution we visited. This institution faced little competition for local students and was unable to serve local demand with its current capacity. Although this college was trying to meet the needs of the population and do what it could to serve those who actually attended the institution, it was not trying to identify new needs or improve the extent to which it was meeting the needs of current students dramatically. As the only game in town, this institution would be hardly impacted by a change in its reputation. Institutions that face the pressure of competition have to work to build their reputations in order to maintain their customer bases.

Many of the strategies pursued by institutions are inherently risky. Risk is particularly evident in prestige seekers. PSs must allocate large amounts of discretionary resources to costly investments in prestige, which have uncertain payoffs. If the payoffs do not materialize, or are long delayed, pressure will grow for the institution to abandon its prestige seeking. If the institution abandons prestige seeking, it must stop maintaining or even dismantle its investments in prestige. The institution will then end up poorer for the failed investments. Reputation-based institutions are less vulnerable than prestige seekers since the investments required to achieve and maintain reputation are smaller than those required to achieve prestige, and the payoffs are more certain and are realized in a shorter amount of time. The smaller investments and more certainty mean that reputation-based institutions face a small chance that they will have to abandon major investments.

Site Visit Examples

Below we present six examples, drawn from our site visits. The first three institutions are financially healthy; the following three are unhealthy. Throughout we refer to them by contrived names. (The terms *university* and *college* are used purely generically and bear no relation to the actual names of the institutions described. We refer to the institutions as *colleges* if they are exclusively or almost exclusively undergraduate. If the institution offers graduate degrees, we call it a *university*). The cases serve to illustrate how each school's strategy is related across revenue markets and the ways that strategies do and do not promote financial health. Following these case studies, Chapter 6 examines data on a wider population of institutions to draw more general conclusions about the relationships among strategy, revenue, expenditure, and financial health.

In Figures 5.1 to 5.6 we will illustrate each institution's choices on the three summary dimensions of position and strategy developed in Figure 3.4. We indicate an institution's present strategy and position by a heavy dot, with past movements indicated by arrows. For simplicity's sake, we do not diagram the scope dimension but rather list the dimensions verbally, together with a square diagram for each institution. The square shows degree level and strategic type (P, PS, or R).

University A: Maintaining a Financially Healthy Prestige Equilibrium

When one first steps onto the campus of University A, its quiet, serene atmosphere, pleasant landscaping, and attractive buildings that complement the surrounding community seem to represent all that one associates with academia. It has a hallowed, studied quality. This outward appearance seems to reflect accurately the healthy state of the school. University A, an independent nonprofit institution located in a residential area of a midsized city, is an example of a thriving prestigious institution; it is a school with a stable strategy that has generated a national standing in all four revenue markets. It offers many examples of the rewards of a P strategy and how to maintain prestige. The strong financial health of the university allows the institution a wide flexibility to choose the type of students it admits, its class sizes, the faculty it hires, and the research areas its faculty pursue.

The major business of University A is research, much of it financed by the federal government. The provost observed that it "is really a research institution with a small university attached." Performance is assessed by reference to how well the school is doing in the research market relative to other universities: it refers to National Research Council rankings, for example. The university has been pursuing this focus for decades. Consequently, its world-renowned faculty members are very active and are granted tenure and promotions on the basis of their research. University A is extremely par-

Figure 5.1
University A Strategy

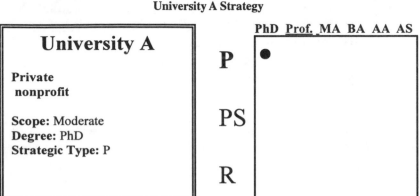

Figure 5.2
University B Strategy

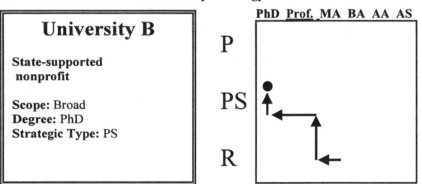

Figure 5.3
College C Strategy

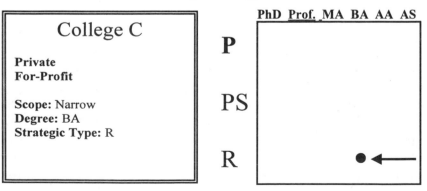

Figure 5.4
University D Strategy

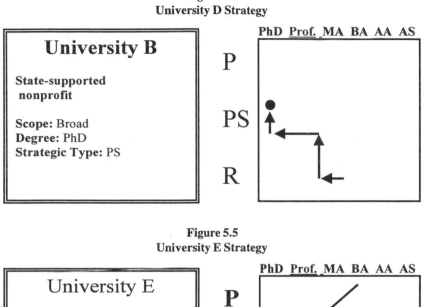

Figure 5.5
University E Strategy

Figure 5.6
College F Strategy

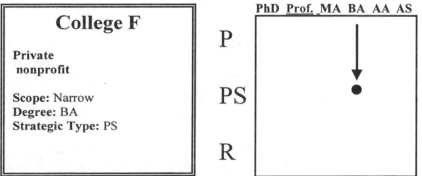

ticular in its hiring of faculty; the primary goal of the hiring process is to maintain the quality of the research program. As the president put it,: "Sometimes we wait five years to hire the 'right' faculty member." Whatever funds are allocated for faculty hiring remain with the department until it fills the position—there is no threat of the funds being taken away if someone is not found right away.

The faculty attract who are the most academically able graduate students from all over the world, excited to work on cutting-edge research. A small class of undergraduates is admitted, and most live on campus, maintaining a tight-knit social life during their studies. The research reputation of the school again allows it to draw the top academic undergraduate students from around the nation. (Undergraduates explained to us that they were attracted by the opportunities to work with the faculty directly.) The university is generous with financial aid, which is used partly to ensure that the most talented students come to the school as well as to help to promote some socioeconomic and racial diversity among the student body. In addition, the university consciously holds tuition slightly below that of comparable private universities and is trying to limit annual increases to no more than 1–2 percent over general inflation.

University A is a specialized institution, limiting the scope of its activities in terms of the disciplines it supports. This has been a strategic choice. It is attempting to maintain strong research programs not in every field, but rather in a selected few. It has recently begun to strengthen its research in an area that is undeveloped but that is still closely related to its core. The senior administrators expressed the goals of University A as "to be the best at whatever we do," "to be a world-class institution, with high-impact research," and to "maintain flexibility: continue with core research, while allocating additional funds for 'seed' projects." The president said, "If you're going to be the best, you have to be on the cutting edge, and you must commit resources to new fields."

The university gets revenue from all four revenue markets and is financially healthy. Its health is illustrated by a number of things: it has no deferred maintenance on its buildings; its endowment is large and growing; it receives significant annual gifts; it has maintained its research revenues in the face of intense competition; and it has recently considered a 25 percent reduction in tuition. The existing high tuition discounts mean that the revenue effect of a tuition cut would be relatively small. Still, it is a tribute to the strong health of the university that there is serious discussion of a major reduction in tuition.

The university's strength comes to a large extent from its endowment. As expected in a prestigious private research university, voluntary giving is significant. The trustees work hard to support the school financially with their own resources and through their contacts. The university is not complacent, however. The president believes that the endowment could easily be doubled in size, especially if declines in federal research funding jeopardize the research work of the university. One strategy for increasing voluntary support is to make alumni feel more involved in the university. Alumni have felt disenfranchised in recent years, but the university is planning more emphasis on alumni relations in the future. (The problem may be inherent in small universities that have not had many staff in alumni support functions.) Another strategy the university is pursuing is development of new sources of revenue through "technology transfer," whereby the institution negotiates for royalties when its discoveries are sold to industry. There are plans to keep even more of the potential payoffs "in house" by initiating a program of internal grants that will allow the university to take ideas "from invention to start-up company." The school has added staff, some with legal expertise and others with finance backgrounds in private equity, to assist the faculty in new start-up ventures. The vice-president for finance added that the university's motivation for going after equity stakes is not just an awareness of the financial potential but anxiety over dependence on federal funding.

In fact, the main challenge facing the school is future competition for federal research sponsorship. Although the university has not been hard hit to date, faculty members are expending more and more resources than ever before to bring in grant money. The vice-president for finance noted that "while the research budget is growing at single-digit rates, the grant writing budget is growing at double-digit rates." As one of the faculty members in our focus group put it, "We're bringing in just as much money as before, but we're writing double the number of proposals to do so."

University A's strategy is to be as eminent as possible in research in order to maintain market share in the event that the overall research market shrinks. Its focus is on "maintaining quality" and its endowment and strong prestige in the student and research markets give it a solid base. It uses its resources strategically by supporting prestige in its main market: conducting long searches for faculty members and hiring the best , providing substantial internal funding and seed money to support new faculty members, and making major investments in junior faculty laboratories, and focusing its efforts in a small number of fields and emphasizing graduate education.

University A is a successful P institution, one that has reaped the benefits of prestige and generated more than ample revenues in private giving and public research dollars. It rewards its faculty with cutting-edge facilities, extensive support, and top-quality students. Further, it demonstrates a sensible strategy of ongoing investments in prestige, protecting itself against potential uncertainties in federal research funding.

University B: Growth and Savvy Management Support Successful Prestige Seeking

University B is an institution in a state of flux. Until recently, it might have been viewed as a typical "second-tier" state university, offering a wide range of programs at the undergraduate and master's levels, focused on providing access to the citizens of its state. More recently, it has switched gears into a more risky prestige-seeking strategy, fueled by the desire to expand its programs and degree offerings and to raise its national profile.

The school is located in a large, growing city. The university is young but has already established several campuses to serve the diverse needs of the metropolitan residents. It is a state-funded institution, part of a state system of universities. This university began with upper division undergraduate and master degree programs. (Undergraduates had to attend community colleges to fulfill their general education requirements then transfer to University B as juniors.) In the early 1980s, the university expanded its educational offerings in two important directions. First, it added a lower-division curriculum with general education and freshmen were admitted to study. Second, shortly after that change, doctoral programs were established. In fact, it has recently shifted to a prestige-seeking strategy in each of its revenue markets: it has not only expanded its degree offerings but also begun to invest in research, sought to develop a nationally recognized football program, and has aggressively challenged the state "flagship" university for public resources.

Consistent with this PS strategy, outside validation of the achievements of the campus is very important. The university has a chapter of Phi Beta Kappa, the national academic honorary society. Chapters are rare in this state, making this external recognition significant. The president also outlined specific, achievable objectives for the whole university: for example, he said he wanted the campus to move from "Research University II" to "Research University I" (in the Carnegie Classification system). This is seen as the "ticket to recognition." External image also played a role in developing a NCAA Division IA football team, another component of this university's PS strategy. It was argued by students and administrators (though not the faculty) that a major sports team would raise campus spirit, give the alumni something to rally around, and bolster fundraising efforts. While the president was initially opposed to the idea, he became convinced that a football team can be a tremendous asset to a public university in a state that values winning football teams. High-level state politicians are often spotted at the home football games of this state's flagship university in the company of the president. Therefore, the football program can support the overall goal of achieving prominence and prestige.

University B is well positioned to pursue a PS strategy. It has a healthy revenue stream and is in the midst of sustained growth in both public funds and private gifts. But financing its growth while attempting to maintain quality is a challenge. So far, the university has succeeded in increasing its public revenue to fund its ongoing growth. Campus funds have recently grown faster than those of any other institution in the state, although there are larger concerns about the state's ability to continue financing the growth of higher education in the face of competing demands on resources. The president said that the state board of regents was trying to "keep the campus down" in favor of the more high-profile flagship. State government attention is focused on the flagship. Because attention is focused elsewhere, the university enjoys some freedom, but it is not taken as seriously as is the flagship by the state legislature. Since the legislature has a very powerful influence over higher education in this state, attracting more positive attention to the campus is viewed as essential to the strategy of the campus.

The university's administrators expressed their goal as gaining national prominence for the campus while serving the local region. Service to the area includes educating students, conducting research relevant to the region, and other community service activities. Both the university and the community place a priority on maintaining close ties. Regional high school graduation rates are increasing and more graduates have college aspirations. The region is advancing economically. For all these reasons, the community has been especially supportive of the university.

The university has made some inroads into establishing prestige in the research arena, but progress has been slow. While departments in some fields compete at the highest level for new faculty members, many good research-oriented faculty members leave, often because of the lack of support (e.g., inadequate numbers of research assistants or shortages of equipment). Many are not comfortable at the university during this transition period, and some said the "academy is in jeopardy." The position of the faculty is not surprising in light of the strong PS strategy of the university.

The university's current president uses a decidedly corporate management style. Vice Presidents are held accountable for specific, measurable goals such as increases in enrollment or fundraising. Salaries and bonuses are dependent upon attaining these goals. VPs who do not perform are dismissed; the president has fired on average one VP each year. Some VPs use a similar management approach with employees in their divisions. The president requires that all goals must be appropriate and relevant to the university's overarching goals of increasing national prominence and service to the local community.

University B has an opportunity to take the increasing revenues from growth and invest in prestige. It has already experienced major success in some of its prestige investments and appears ready to continue building prestige. There is faculty resentment because of the heavy, single-minded focus on these investments, but as the university achieves greater prestige, it will likely have increased revenues to compensate the faculty. This university is financially healthy while pursuing a PS strategy. That is a combination that few institutions can manage.

College C: A Profitable, Customer-Oriented, Innovative School with a Good Reputation

College C is a dramatically different type of higher education institution. It is one of a growing number of highly visible, for-profit entities, aggressively expanding in entrepreneurial fashion into clearly identifiable markets where the opportunities for economic success are greatest. It has many campuses all over the country. In the past, most of the college's students earned two-year degrees or certificates. Today the college is emphasizing degree programs, particularly expanding the programs offering bachelor's degrees.

This institution is different from traditional nonprofits in many ways. For example, it typically has just one building per campus, and campuses are located mainly in suburban and urban middle-class areas all over the country. It has none of the trappings of a traditional college—no dormitories; few social gathering areas; no tenured, full-time faculty; little student activity—with functional space that is heavily used. One administrator commented, that while other institutions "create campuses," College C "runs a business."

The college is highly centralized, with major decisions affecting each campus made at the headquarters level. The president appears to set the goals, taking into consideration the expectations of the shareholders and college and university accreditors. Individual campuses and their associated advisory boards provide input to tailor programs to the needs and opportunities of the local environment. The central office conducts elaborate analyses before choosing the location for a new campus. The college tends to locate near major highways to make the college accessible to as many potential students as possible; they prefer to locate in industrial parks to minimize the development that they have to undertake in starting and maintaining a campus.

It pursues a reputation-based strategy, primarily offering two-year and four-year undergraduate degrees in specific fields of study. Its reputation is based primarily on its demonstrated ability to prepare students for employment and place them successfully in good jobs. The college's mission is "to provide the highest-quality educational instruction which prepares students for employment in the field in which they study." Students attend classes forty-eight weeks a year. With three shifts of students attending from morning until night, facilities are used sixteen hours a day.

The college claims that it has an easier time meeting expectations than do traditional, nonprofit colleges. The college is clear that "customer service" is their objective, wherein *customer* means both students and employers.[1] The college identifies top employer needs to guide its educational offerings. To meet employer demands, College C focuses on experiential learning, accomplished by putting students in a laboratory environment. Overall, students spend about

60 percent of their time in the classroom, learning "theory," and the other 40 percent of their time in the lab, learning through hands-on problem solving. All courses include both theory and lab components, which are often taught by the same instructor. The application of theory to practical lab work is the central pedagogical goal in all of the programs.

The faculty at College C is different from faculties at traditional nonprofit colleges. Faculty members teach twenty-six hours per week. Because the curriculum is determined centrally, faculty members spend a minimal amount of time preparing lecture notes or deciding what to teach. Curriculum development is centralized in the system headquarters. There is a single curriculum for each degree program. In these ways, the college makes the faculty focus solely on the process of delivering education in the classroom. The faculty spend little, if any, time on research.

Success is measured by two important numbers: student enrollment and placement rates. The enrollment numbers tell management what future revenues will be. Placement rates are the most crucial factor in attracting students. Feedback from employers is also important. Both when designing a new curriculum—and when refining an existing one—the college solicits input from employers, including those that already hire its graduates and those who do not.

College C considers itself almost immune from competition, in large part because of the accreditation system. Since the college has been accredited for decades, it enjoys a tremendous advantage over potential new competitors. According to a senior administrator, accrediting bodies effectively limit any competition from new institutions and, as such, represent "one of the greatest barriers to entry" in the educational market. In addition to these regulatory barriers, the college system enjoys significant economies of scale because of its nationwide network of campuses. It is able to spread the costs of centralized management and curriculum development across its campuses. The system faces competition from public institutions, although indirectly. Because of College C's year-round schedule, students are guaranteed completion of a bachelor's degree in three years. The carefully planned programs mean that students can get the courses they need when they need them. Although public colleges have an apparent advantage in low tuition, College C emphasizes its rapid three-year completion of the bachelor's degree, thanks to year-round class schedules. The focused curriculum appeals to students who have had some trouble with the traditional learning environment.

College C's leaders appear extremely confident about the health of their institution. The system is well positioned relative to traditional institutions in terms of placement rates, quick degree completion, and the ability to serve the needs of nontraditional students. The college straddles two different identities: a leader in nontraditional education and a legitimate institution of higher education. Hence, while it promotes the work experience of its faculty, it must also ensure that the education meets more traditional measures of quality. College C highlights its accreditation status in its brochures. Not only does the literature state that all of its campuses are accredited (or are seeking accreditation), but the catalog explains what accreditation means for the college—that its "curricula, facilities, equipment and staff satisfy the guidelines established for institutions of higher learning."

In summary, College C pursues its R strategy efficiently and skillfully. The centralized decision-making structure makes it relatively easy for a few administrators to set goals and allocate resources. It has no traditional faculty vying for consumption benefits and a student body focused on acquiring usable skills as speedily as possible. It has established a market niche and expanded geographically with thorough planning. College C is run like a business and is a financially healthy one.

University D: Financially Unhealthy Prestige Seeker Struggling to Overcome Location

In contrast to our first three cases, we now examine several schools that are struggling. They illustrate the inherent dilemmas and risk of a PS resource allocation strategy and its effects on financial health. University D's problems stem partly from its location: it was established in an economically disadvantaged region, in an unattractive section of a midsized city. University D is statefunded and part of a system of highly regarded universities, but as one of the more recently established schools in the system, it has always suffered from a "backwater" image. The university has been a PS institution since its founding.

The school has a full range of undergraduate and graduate programs, but it is a small school by the standards of public universities. Therefore, University D can offer students a "personal touch." Students at the school have more access to faculty and greater opportunities to become involved in research as undergraduates than is typical. Students have little trouble enrolling in classes they want or need and those classes are taught by faculty members rather than by graduate students. University D originally wanted to be the "Swarthmore of the West." However, the school usually ranks last among the state system's campuses in terms of the average SAT scores and grades of entering students. It also has a more disadvantaged student population, with many students being the first in their families to attend college. Despite this, University D has the lowest time to degree and highest graduation rates of all the state's universities, indicating that it may be doing a great job with the poorest material. There seems to be little payoff for this in the student market though, as its location and lack of prestige within the state system depresses student interest in attending the university. In the face of this problem, the university's approach is community outreach—interviewees say want to work with the local junior high and high schools to raise the educational and economic level of the surrounding community. In this way they hope to build a base of qualified students in the local area from which they can draw. However, there is little real sense that this is an aggressive, viable strategy.

One component of this institution's PS resource allocation strategy is to expand enrollment. In the past, the state system has approved expansion plans for the system, but each time growth was directed to other campuses. Administrators believe that the time is right for University D to grow, but such a strategy is in direct conflict with the benefits associated with being a small campus. A further complication is that facilities are already used heavily and the campus is operating at close to its capacity. And, while the campus was established relatively recently, a great deal of building maintenance has been neglected. We were told that this is a serious problem and that "the buildings are falling down around us."

These problems in the student market are compounded by a desire to become a major research player. Administrators at University D would like to have the prestige associated with a major research university. They already claimed to compare favorably with similarly sized institutions such as Vanderbilt University and University of Rochester. Thinking of the heavy competition in research markets, some administrators said that University D is like a "ma and pa grocery store" trying to break into a market dominated by national chains. Research labs are inadequate, and they have problems attracting top faculty members.

University D recruits faculty with Ph.D.s nationally from "the best schools." However, they noted that they tend to get people who value teaching as well, since the university is not a high-profile research institution. Because of several trends, faculty members are becoming more disengaged from campus life. Dual-career couples prefer to live closer to major metropolitan centers, where spouses have access to more jobs. As a result, faculty members spend more time commuting and less time on the campus. The president's desire to demonstrate faculty productivity has encouraged the faculty to emphasize structured activities related to teaching and research. Faculty members are reducing time devoted to unstructured activities that promote interaction between students and faculty.

University D has ambitions in both the student and research markets, but it is not at all clear that such aspirations are feasible. University D demonstrates how a state-funded university develops poor financial health. The university's strategy of prestige seeking through growth is incompatible with its circumstances. Growth threatens to destroy the very qualities of the university that it seems to prize: its small, intimate community. And growth is constrained by an undesirable location and low pecking order among the state's campuses. While interviewees hope to receive more funding for students (and are increasing their enrollment even before the additional money is appropriated) the state is unlikely to provide resources to build new facilities. They hope to rely on private sector money for facilities but have no realistic plan for achieving this. With no sources of capital for new buildings and questionable commitments to pay increased operating expenses, University D is financially unhealthy.

University E: Expansion into Research Jeopardizing Financial Health

While University D illustrates how the constraints of location and public status affect the viability of a prestige-seeking strategy, University E is an excellent example of a private school that has been following a prestige-seeking resource allocation strategy following an aggressive attempt at expansion. University E sacrificed some of its historic prestige in the undergraduate student market when it expanded the scope of its academic and degree offerings and made forays into the research market. The institution is currently searching for a new identity that it can support financially. The experience of University E illustrates the risks associated with expansion for P institutions and the difficulty of using faculty research to help attract higher-quality students and hence improve prestige.

University E, an independent nonprofit institution, started as a classic undergraduate college. It possesses a very attractive campus with stately older buildings and beautiful grounds. The campus is located in a small suburban community. The university once enjoyed a high level of prestige stemming from its outstanding undergraduate educational program. It competed nationally for, and attracted its share of, the nation's brightest students. It still compares itself with the most prestigious undergraduate colleges in the country, although after a disappointing ranking in *U.S. News & World Report* it has developed a "benchmarking set" that includes some less prestigious institutions as well. Although it has expanded its degree offerings to the Ph.D. level and engages in a modest level of research, University E shares a liberal arts and student-centered focus with other prestigious undergraduate colleges. Students we talked to praised the school's atmosphere—the friendliness of fellow students, the open attitudes that prevail, and the ability to "organize a group for anything you want." Almost all students live on campus. Small classes, taught by faculty members, also got high marks from students. One student noted that "professors get to teach what they love, so they have lots of enthusiasm."

In attempting to maintain its prestige in the student market, University E has faced increasing and intense competition for top students, many of whom also apply to universities with a more substantial and established research emphasis. As is the case at many similar colleges, this competition for students has driven University E to offer large tuition discounts in order to attract the best students. In the past decade, the tuition discounts threatened to push the university's budget into deficit. But after recently analyzing its finances, the school has cut back its tuition discounting significantly and reduced the size of its faculty and staff. University E maintains its commitment to need-blind admissions but has moved away from this ideal in spirit if not in reality by significantly increasing the number of students it accepts through "early decision" programs, in which the applicants pledge to withdraw all other applications if they are accepted early to the school. In 1996, over one-third of the admission offers were made through the early decision program, and these applicants are much less likely to be financially needy. Hence, a larger number of slots are being committed upfront to a wealthier population. In addition, financial concerns have prompted the school to increase significantly the proportion of student aid comprised of loans as opposed to institutional scholarships. The president expressed concern that this policy was placing a serious burden on students and making his institution unattractive to middle-income families. These financial realities are jeopardizing the university's commitment to a diverse student body.

Problems with funding students arise in large part because of the endowment-funded expansion of the school's programs, faculty, and student body in the 1960s and 1970s. According to one administrator, the institution "expended its endowment base too rapidly and at the wrong time." In the late 1960s, this institution had one of the largest endowments per student among liberal arts colleges and endowment revenue paid two-thirds of instructional costs. Now, revenue from endowment covers only one-third of instructional costs.

University E's expansion was multidimensional. The primary objective appears to have been expanding the scope of the institution by building programs in new areas such as studio arts and the sciences. In addition, the institution added graduate programs in many areas and began to encourage faculty research. Complementing this academic expansion was a high level of construction activity; several new dormitories and academic buildings were built during this time.

These expenditures have made a much broader curriculum available to students. Today the school offers forty-five undergraduate majors, many more than do competing liberal arts colleges. Even this number reflects recent reductions. According to a faculty member, "We used to have a lot more programs—I was amazed at how many balls we could keep in the air." Another faculty member summed up the university's evolution: "We sold our endowment to develop a richer curriculum." However, the expansion was costly to the institution in a way that seriously impacts its ability to maintain prestige in the undergraduate student market. By 1980, the institution had an endowment that, in the view of one administrator, "was 30 percent of what it should have been" relative to the most prestigious liberal arts competitors. Endowment revenue is crucial to allowing the institution to attract the highest-quality students.

In addition, University E's encouragement of faculty research, perhaps originally intended only as a complement to a quality undergraduate education, has led to some tensions that are commonly observed in institutions striving for prestige in the research market. The university now finds itself with a faculty that takes research seriously and that largely rejects the "liberal arts college" view of the school. Faculty members are well rewarded with low teaching loads, good students and colleagues, and generous sabbatical leave policies. Recently, as the university has struggled financially, faculty members have complained about "underfunding" in research, pressure to increase departmental enrollment, and consequently increasing class sizes. Over the past five years, the school has downsized the faculty by fifteen positions (three faculty per year) and implemented two early retirement programs for staff. Students and faculty both complain that faculty reductions are increasing the size of classes. Some faculty members believe that the faculty has been made a "scapegoat" for the school's problems by administration, parents, and students.

University E thus finds itself caught part way between returning to its past as a prestigious undergraduate liberal arts school and sustaining the more expansive "little university." For many years, the leadership of this institution has failed to choose between these two visions. This failure to choose has led to increasing frustration on the part of the faculty and doubtful long-run financial viability. The university has recently appointed a new president, whose number-one priority is to clarify the direction of the university. In the president's own words, "We need to get a mission for the institution." The school is also embarking on a major capital campaign, after years of complacency about the health of its endowment.

University E shows the risks of expanded scope for an endowed private institution. Investments in new programs and in research activities are expensive. Although the expansion was viewed as an investment in the quality of the undergraduate program, given potential synergy between teaching and research, it appears to have been a costly and troubled resource allocation strategy. Now the university faces the difficult choice of deciding whether to narrow the institutional scope and trim research and graduate programs despite the broad support for such activities on the part of the faculty. Even if it makes that choice, it will face stiff competition from prestigious undergraduate colleges that did not spend down their endowments in the interest of expansion.[2] University E has no assurance that it will ever regain the prestige it sacrificed.

College F: Prestige Seeker with Expensive Ambitions

College F, an independent nonprofit institution, is a green oasis in the midst of a mixed urban and residential section of a large metropolitan area. The college had strong prestige in its local area based on its undergraduate education program. Many prominent local leaders were educated at College F. The college's prestige has been eroded over the past decade or so, such that it is now appropriately seen as a prestige seeker. College F is a particularly interesting case, but its problems have not come as a result of an attempt to expand its programs or enter heavily into research. Changes in the external environment and other internal changes have been the culprit. Now it is vying to regain the prestige it has lost, competing in a wider national market.

The college's lost prestige resulted, in part, from external forces. Since the 1970s, the college has faced increasing competition from state universities. Middle-class families are encouraging their children to attend prestigious state universities, where the tuition charges are much lower than they are at College F. This shift has affected the college's ability to attract the most talented students. Students who seek to pursue their educations at elite schools see College F as the lesser school within this group of schools and choose the "better" institutions. As a result, key indicators of prestige for an undergraduate college competing in the student market, such as admission selectivity, have slipped.

Part of the reason for the decline can be traced to the college's mission. Unlike University E, College F has a clear overarching goal, one that was easily articulated by the president and all administrators at the college: excellence in undergraduate education with social equity within the context of an "urban" setting (often used as a code word for *diverse* or *multicultural*). *Excellence* was broadly defined as a high-caliber liberal arts education, and *equity* denoted providing access to students from a diverse set of backgrounds and communities. In the past, the college did not emphasize its metropolitan location to prospective students; now the metropolitan area is seen as attracting out-of-area students. Simultaneously, the campus models itself on the elite liberal arts colleges as it also attempts to be a role model for other schools through its commitment to equity and excellence. The inherent irony results in clashes of ideology and values. The campus wants to be a place where the best and brightest choose to go, but it also wants to challenge traditional, narrowly defined sets of indicators. Administrators recognize that it strives to be and look like other institutions, but the fact that the campus is doing something different means that College F does not "look as good on paper."[3]

The college has attempted to maintain its student body quality, but this is expensive, requiring tuition discounting and aggressive marketing. Financial aid is a significant cost for the campus, especially given its commitment to diversity: 70 percent of students receive financial aid, mostly need based. Since 1983, financial aid has grown, but student applications and enrollments have dropped and dramatically so in the past five years. The loss in net tuition income alone amounts to about $1 million each year or 2.5 percent of the operating budget.

The five years of College F's budget deficit have been financed through the quasi-endowment (accumulated prior savings). As a result of this strategy, the financial statements appear balanced, but the school is not in a long-run equilibrium. Leaders lamented the campus's financial situation. At the most general level, it was acknowledged that the campus has an ambitious and costly mission; given that, a lack of budgetary constraints led to the deficit. Part of the problem resulted from an increase in the number of full-time faculty members by 30 percent in less than a decade. With student numbers remaining the same, the student-faculty ratio decreased by 30 percent. Financial exigencies are also attributable to risky investments in the endowment that did not pay off well, especially investments in the real estate of the region. The endowment of College F is large enough to cushion it from immediate danger, but it is insufficient to maintain the college at its current size. If the college cannot increase tuition revenue, or chooses not to do so, it will have to reduce its faculty and student body to allow it to maintain its operations without depleting the purchasing power of its endowment further.

Alumni giving provides vital support for College F's budget. But many alumni have expressed concern about the direction of the college and are quite vocal about their fondness for the "good old days." The alumni remember fondly their experiences with athletics and fraternities but believe that these values are neglected in the campus's current emphasis on multiculturalism. Alumni giving appears to be highly responsive to issues on campus; for example, when externally visible crosses were removed from the campus chapel located at the entrance to the school, alumni giving dropped noticeably. Alumni have pressured the campus to move in more vocational directions by adding business or law schools, but the campus leadership has resisted. Similarly, fundraising from foundations has been problematic: they are not satisfied with College F's statistics (indicators such as the number of students who applied, their SAT scores, and GPAs), since they do not measure up to the nationally prestigious colleges.

So College F is in a tricky position brought about by its desire to fulfill a very ambitious mission and mismanagement of resources in the past. Funding such a strategy requires increased private giving or tuition revenue, but the latter is in conflict with the goals of the college regarding social equity and diversity and the former is tough because the main givers are alumni who do not like the college's new focus. College F faces an uncertain future.

The Effect of Prestige Seeking on Financial Health

The six case studies bring out a number of interesting lessons on the financial health of individual institutions, the resource allocation strategies institutions pursue, and the nature and implications of competition in this industry. In this section, we recap those lessons and indicate how they apply to a range of institutions beyond the twenty-six we visited. In addition, we examine some statistics on a larger group of institutions. These data demonstrate that many principles illustrated by the case studies are, in fact, applicable to the broad spectrum of colleges and universities in the U.S. higher education industry.

The Relationship of Resource Allocation Strategy to Financial Health

As our examples illustrate, financially healthy institutions (Universities A and B and College C) can be found among those following P, PS, and R resource allocation strategies. The three financially healthy institutions encompass substantial variation on the other two dimensions of strategy as well. They include a very broad university, a narrow university, and a narrow college. The three healthy institutions include an undergraduate-focused college, a comprehensive university moving into graduate education and research, and an established research university. What these institutions have in common is that the strategy they are pursuing is realistic given the competitive environment in which they find themselves. Several of the financially healthy institutions we visited had recently changed their strategy in response to changes in the market for students.

The examples of financially unhealthy institutions span a smaller range of types. It is no coincidence that all three of our financially unhealthy institution examples follow a PS resource allocation strategy. The PS strategy endangers financial health because it forces schools to straddle two worlds. They must meet enough of the external demands to bring in revenue from present customers while making large investments in prestige-building activities. Some of the unhealthy PS institutions we visited were former P schools struggling to maintain prestige in the face of changes in the competitive environment. Others never had prestige but were trying to build it or were trying to expand their scope and degree offerings while maintaining prestige.

When an institution possesses prestige but is striving to expand into more costly degree offerings, it risks current prestige against a mere chance that it will achieve prestige in a broader strategy. As in the case of University E, this may mean that the institution ends up sacrificing its prestige because it is unable to achieve its goals and is unable to regain its former prestige. Since prestigious private schools often have sizable endowments, the risk of expanding prestige is a depleted endowment. University F is likely "overspending" its endowment as it strives to regain lost prestige.

Institutions that pursue prestige without any established prestige risk less, but they can certainly jeopardize financial health. The case of University D shows that even an institution that does not sacrifice present prestige or endowment must sacrifice other discretionary resources to make investments in the areas targeted to enhance prestige. As a result of its need for investments in prestige, University D cannot invest in the reputation-enhancing programs that draw in its current undergraduate students. If the university's investments in prestige do not pay off, the university may find itself unable to generate revenue from the undergraduate student market.

In addition to seeking prestige, colleges and universities face pressure to move along the other two dimensions of strategy. There is pressure to add more programs to become a broader school. There is pressure to offer higher degrees and emphasize research. University B has added new programs, increased its offering of master's and Ph.D. degrees, and shifted its focus toward research. University E has also made these moves. These examples are indeed typical of the movements that higher education institutions make in the United States.

Universities B and E have been able to make these moves because they had sources of funding for investments in prestige and new programs. In University B, the investments were and are funded by growth in state appropriations and tuition as the institution grows to serve more undergraduates. In University E, the investments were funded from the large endowment of the school. Yet institutions without such sources of funding face the same pressures. College F faculty and administrators cited these very same pressures, although they have moved only slightly in their strategy. (College F has added some modest research facilities to its primarily instructional mission.)

Although there is little definitive information on the actual cost of research activities, it is clear from the case studies of Universities A, B, D, and E that the costs of building and maintaining a high-quality research infrastructure—personnel, labs, libraries, and equipment— are large. These cases also illustrate that federal research funding is an important element of research prestige and that competition for this funding is increasing. As a result, institutions concerned with prestige in the research market are driven to subsidize this research activity with other funds in order to reduce the perceived cost to the government and increase their chances of receiving this funding.[4] PS institutions have the strongest incentive to compete for federal funding on the basis of cost because they have less current prestige. The question of whether institutions use tuition revenue to subsidize research activities is less clear.[5] Public institutions can use state resources to leverage federal research funding but are now also starting to attract private donations to a greater extent.

Pressures to seek prestige, offer higher degrees, emphasize research, and expand program offerings arise from many stakeholders: students, faculty, administrators, and state legislators. Students have varied demands, and to attract and retain students, institutions consider new programs. Faculty members often push institutions to emphasize research. Most faculty members are trained in Ph.D. programs in research universities. During their training, these faculty members are socialized to prize academic research (see Massy and Goldman, 1995). But most faculty jobs are not in research-intensive schools. At schools without a past focus on research, new faculty members often push institutions in this direction.

In addition, faculty labor markets value research above teaching ability. Research, with refereed publications, is readily transferable as a faculty credential from institution to institution. Research products make getting a job easier. But teaching skill is not transferable in the same way. While some institutions greatly value teaching, it is much harder to have an objective evaluation of teaching skill than it is of research. Therefore, faculty hiring tends to be based on research even at many institutions that do not focus on research. College F is a good example. The school has moved a little toward research emphasis, pushed by individual faculty members who recognize the importance of research products for their own career enhancement. Faculty and administrators pursue prestige because prestigious institutions have a degree of autonomy from market forces. This autonomy gives freedom of action plus greater consumption benefits. Faculty members are the main beneficiaries, although students likely benefit from a higher labor market payoff.[6]

Both public and private institutions experience increased revenues in the four key revenue markets with increased prestige. We examine some data on revenues in the four markets to extend this observation to a broader class of institutions than is represented by the ones that we were able to visit. Figure 5.7 presents data for private colleges that focus on undergraduate education. (All revenue amounts are scaled on a per-faculty-member basis to make comparison among schools of different sizes easier.) The upper panel of the figure shows two groups, 1 and 2, located on our strategy diagram.[7] Both groups focus on undergraduate education, but Group 2 is more prestigious. The figure shows the large increase in private giving between Group 1 and Group 2. Prestige translates directly into power in the private giving market. These colleges receive essentially zero revenue from public fiscal support (not shown on the graph) and very little from research funding. What may be surprising is that revenue from student enrollments changes little between the two groups. The sticker price of tuition is much higher in Group 2, but other factors mitigate this difference. Specifically, Group 2 faculty members teach less and

Group 2 schools offer larger tuition discounts. As a result, net tuition revenue per faculty member is approximately unchanged with increased prestige.

Many states also implicitly or explicitly reward prestige and a broad scope of academic programs with higher state appropriations per student. Across all types of state-supported universities, the more prestigious receive higher appropriations. Figure 5.8 depicts similar data for state-supported universities. These institutions are divided into four groups, based on degree offerings and research. For simplicity's sake, Figure 5.8 shows only the degree dimension. Group 1 is generally broad scope universities offering bachelor's and master's degrees. These institutions are pursuing a reputation-based resource allocation strategy. Group 2 universities are pursuing a prestige-seeking strategy, offering some doctoral degrees and pursuing research. Group 3 universities are also pursuing a prestige-seeking resource allocation strategy, offering more doctoral degrees and conducting more research than those in Group 2. Group 4 contains prestigious research universities, with major research emphasis and a large volume of sponsored research.[8] For these universities, sponsored research funding practically defines prestige. This association is borne out in the data, quite dramatically. Research funding increases steadily from Group 1 to Group 4. In Group 4, it exceeds all other revenue sources. The increase in public fiscal support is also noteworthy. States appear to appropriate more funding to more prestigious universities. The increase is steady and sizable from Group 1 to 4. Private giving is much smaller in this set of schools, but it also displays strong and steady increases from Group 1 to Group 4.

Revenue from student enrollments barely increases with prestige. Compared to the increases in the other three revenue markets, the increase in net tuition is unimportant. As in the private colleges, possibly higher posted tuition rates are offset by lower faculty teaching loads and greater tuition discounts. For private colleges of any type, tuition revenues are very important. Since private R institutions receive almost all of their revenue from tuition, they are often called *tuition-driven* schools. The tuition-driven schools (private R) must be extremely responsive to students and their needs. College C is an example of such a school, and since it is for profit, the administration is even more focused on the need to respond quickly and well to student and employer demands. College C has been mark-

Figure 5.7
Revenues Increase with Prestige in Private Undergraduate Colleges

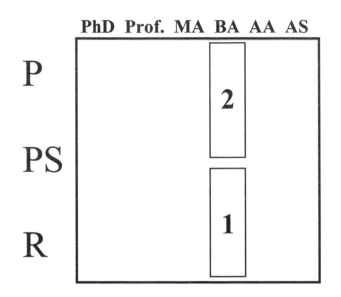

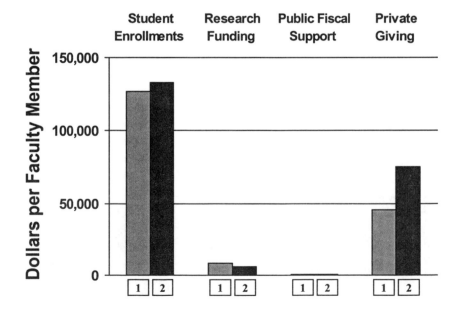

Figure 5.8
Revenues Increase with Prestige in State Universities

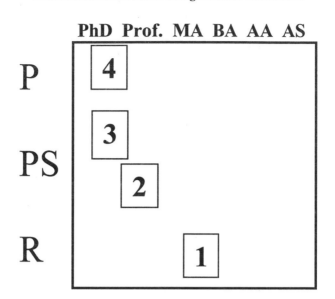

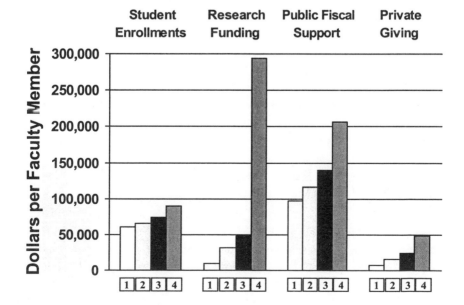

edly successful in developing educational programs that are precisely responsive to employment opportunities, and thus to student demands. Nonprofit, private R schools also often behave like College C. Another institution we visited is a nonprofit university that competes head on with for-profit colleges and universities. This university delivers career-focused education at nights and on weekends when working students can attend. The reliance on tuition makes this university very responsive to the demands and wants of students.

Public R institutions are similar to private R schools, except that with the former state governments play a large role. Many state governments are increasing their demands for their universities to respond more rapidly and thoroughly to the career needs of students, especially those state-funded universities that focus on associate's, bachelor's, or master's degrees. For these institutions, tuition and state appropriations make up almost all of their revenue. When students express demands that are backed by the state legislature or governing board, the state-funded R institutions respond clearly.

A notable feature of revenues, as shown on the figures, is that the more prestigious universities or colleges do not experience higher tuition revenues along with their prestige. It is certainly common for more prestigious schools to have a higher sticker price for tuition. But these higher sticker prices are offset by greater tuition discounts and lower faculty teaching loads. Thus, as University B enhances its prestige, it should not expect that tuition revenue (adjusted for size) will increase much, if at all. But the university will be gaining financial flexibility as it is able to offer more financial aid to attract desirable students, further enhancing its prestige and faculty satisfaction. In addition, the consumption rewards of prestige will enable University B to reduce faculty teaching loads.

Costs and Faculty Power

Prestige is associated with increased consumption by institutions' internal constituencies, particularly faculty. The rewards of prestige, for example, often entail reducing faculty teaching loads and increasing faculty salaries. These responses have important implications for the costs of producing higher education. The costs of production, in turn, influence the prices that students and governments must pay for higher education's services.

Overall, faculty labor costs are the single most important cost of production. The faculty represent's a powerful interest in almost every institution. In many institutions, the faculty is unionized.[9] But even without a union, the faculty is often the principal determiner of institutional strategy. Many public institutions have mandated shared governance arrangements. The one segment of the industry where the faculty has little power is in some private, for-profit and nonprofit R institutions, like College C. College C treats faculty like ordinary labor, not as part of the governance of the college. Similarly, one private, nonprofit R institution operates almost exclusively with part-time faculty members. These part-timers teach one or two courses for a fixed fee per course. They have no status within the institution; the institution is operated by a few administrators.

This faculty power has enormous implications for the costs of producing higher education's services. Many of the officials we interviewed expressed strong concerns about the continued rise in costs of operating their institutions. But at one prestigious university, the approach to "dealing with the cost problem" is to focus on administrative efficiency rather than instructional costs. An administrator at this university justified this by pointing out that "the kind of education we do here is so apprenticeship-related that we probably won't drive down teaching costs." This administrator means that students working with faculty in small classes is seen as essential to the school's educational program. With such a perspective, the faculty is not a potential source of productivity improvement. While some productivity gains may come from administrative efficiencies, the bulk of the costs are tied up in faculty and faculty support. Without touching these, this university is unlikely to stem the rise in the costs of production.

At universities with less reverence for the apprenticeship model, faculty members often instruct students in large lectures. Even at these institutions, the power of faculty ensures that there is rarely serious emphasis on reducing faculty payrolls, except in time of the direst fiscal emergency. Indeed, faculty tenure can be abrogated only in a formally declared financial exigency or when an entire department is closed. The president of one undergraduate college we visited acknowledged that, while the concept of "productivity" comes easily to the board of trustees, it is anathema to the faculty.

The power of faculty influences the cost structure of almost all higher education institutions. It is true that the costs of operation vary with the strategy an institution pursues. Overall costs increase in broader, larger schools and in those pursuing a prestige-based or prestige-seeking resource allocation strategy. But even adjusting for the different sizes of institutions, P institutions face higher costs than do other types. Looking at faculty salaries in particular, the national data demonstrate that faculty costs increase with the prestige of the institutions. The higher faculty salaries are evident in both private and public institutions. Figures 5.9 and 5.10 show the same sets of institutions as are shown in the earlier analyses of revenue streams. Figure 5.9 shows that faculty salaries in the more prestigious, private undergraduate colleges are 38 percent higher than they are in their less prestigious counterparts. The public universities show a steady increase in salaries from Group 1 to Group 4, representing an overall difference of 28 percent shown in Figure 5.10.

Higher revenues are generated from a successful prestige-seeking strategy. But there is a great deal of risk and uncertain payoff; there are also increasing costs. Why then do we see so many institutions pursuing such strategies? In general, it seems that faculty members (and in some cases future students and the federal government) benefit from a prestige-based resource allocation strategy. They benefit through lower teaching loads, higher salaries, and improved research facilities. The faculty, however, does not pay the true costs of this resource allocation behavior—rather, private donors, state governments, and students bear the burden.[10]

Much public attention has focused recently on the rise in higher education prices to students. Tuition has risen more than 250 percent over the past fifteen years (1980-1995) compared to a little under 90 percent for the Consumer Price Index. The increase in tuition has been driven in part by the desire of institutions to generate greater revenues to fund financial aid for some students. It has also come about in order to overcome increasing costs of production in higher education. The Higher Education Price Index, which estimates the cost of the basket of goods and services typically purchased by the industry, rose 426 percent between 1966 and 1995 compared to 376 percent for all prices over the same period. This increase is attributable in part to rising labor costs through salaries and reduced teaching loads.

Figure 5.9
Costs Increase with Prestige in Private Undergraduate Colleges

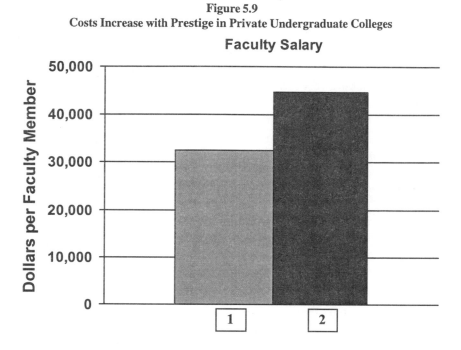

Figure 5.10
Costs Increase with Prestige in State Universities

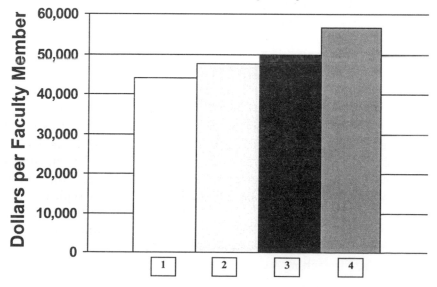

When the Faculty Has Less Power

For-profit colleges have focused increasing attention on the role of faculty in higher education. A primary distinction can be made between institutions that offer tenure to faculty members who have demonstrated a record of accomplishment and those institutions that do not. We visited four institutions that do not offer tenure to faculty. Two of these are for-profit colleges; two are nonprofit universities. Although they offer different educational programs to different markets, there are important similarities among them regarding their relationships to faculty. These institutions differ markedly from traditional colleges and universities in curriculum development, faculty schedules, faculty employment status, and relations between faculty and administration.

The faculty in traditional institutions is responsible for the development of curriculum. For the most part, this means that an individual faculty member is responsible for the content of the course he/she teaches. Occasionally, there are collaborations or committees that work to identify a set of core courses to be offered by a department, to establish basic guidelines for the content of key courses, or to link important elements of a curriculum. However, faculty members still retain a great deal of latitude to structure their courses within these parameters. The for-profit institutions we visited operate in an entirely different way. In these places, curriculum development is divorced from teaching. There is a single standard curriculum for each degree program and every course within it. These curricula are developed by a team of specialists in elaborate processes at the home offices of these institutions. At one of these institutions, the centralized curriculum development process is so complete that faculty members have to spend only a minimal amount of time preparing lecture notes. At the other, faculty members must do slightly more work to prepare for teaching since they have some discretion in teaching methods and a small part of each course is reserved for topics decided by the faculty at each local site.

Recall that the degree programs at these for-profit institutions are highly regimented and oriented toward preparing the student for a particular type of employment. Once the student selects his or her degree program, nearly all of the individual courses are determined by the institution. This regularity in curricula has benefits to certain students and especially employers. But it is a quite different way of operating an institution of higher education—compared to the smorgasbord approach followed at traditional colleges and universities.

By defining faculty positions to include teaching duties to the exclusion of research and curriculum development, the for-profit institutions are able to have faculty in the classroom as much as twenty-six hours per week. Such a teaching burden represents at least two or three times what would be expected in a conventional college or university term. In addition, faculty members at these for-profits work a twelve-month schedule, teaching three semesters instead of the standard two.

Faculty members are not permitted to leave campus during the term. Leave for personal or professional reasons must be scheduled during the one, two, or three-week breaks between semesters. Administrators do recognize that this policy restricts their faculties from participating in scholarly conferences and other professional activities that help faculty members stay current in their fields. Because the constraint may affect the faculty's value to the institution, administrators are considering some modification to the leave policy, though any modification clearly clashes with their view of faculty's employment status.

Managers of these for-profits are clearly running business operations. To maintain flexibility in the face of changing student markets, these institutions do not grant tenure or long-term contracts for faculty members. Faculty members are employees, inputs into the production process, exactly like staff members. They hold no special place within the institution and are not responsible for its governance. However, faculty members at these institutions can and do become shareholders in the company. In this way, they can become stakeholders in the institution, but they are accorded no special privileges due to their status as faculty independent of their shareholdings.

The nonprofit institutions we visited that do not grant tenure show some characteristics of the for-profits as well as some characteristics of traditional tenure-based institutions. Although faculty members do not receive tenure, full-time faculty members are granted multiyear contracts with a specific review prior to the contracts' expiration. The duration of these contracts varies, based on seniority and other factors, up to seven years at one of the institutions and up to three years at the other. At these schools, unlike the for-profits, full-time faculty formally participate in the governance of the enterprise and academic freedom and scholarship are specifically recognized in the standards for faculty. Although these institutions do grant full-time faculty some of the rights and privileges associated with traditional institutions, it should be noted that the full-time faculty constitute a minority (and at one institution less than 10 percent of the total faculty are full-time). Part-time faculty get none of these benefits and essentially serve as a highly flexible labor input. Teaching loads are somewhat lower than they are at the for-profits, with greater responsibility for curriculum development and research. But the management attitudes of senior administrators are very similar to those of the for-profit managers. Managers at the nonprofits, like those at the for-profits, treated their enterprises as businesses.

The discussion in this section highlights the dual role that faculty plays in institutions of higher education. In all institutions, faculty members are suppliers of labor, similar to workers in any other industry; they are paid by institutions to teach, perform research, and provide other sorts of services. In most institutions, they are also stakeholders, with a direct role in the governance of the institution, including decisions about how resources are distributed within the institution and how the institution is run. The extent to which faculty participate in the governance process varies dramatically across institutions. In a recent essay on the American professorate, Clark (1997) suggests that faculty authority is high in institutions with the highest level of prestige but that faculty authority decreases and managerialism increases as prestige declines. We would stress that the role of faculty also depends on the strategy of the institution, not just its current level of prestige. Faculty members are extremely important inputs to investing in prestige and, therefore, are in a better bargaining position in institutions that are interested in maintaining or pursuing prestige (i.e., both P and PS institutions). R institutions do not value the potential contribution of faculty to prestige, and as a result,faculty power is lower at these schools than it is at P and PS institutions. R institutions take a variety of approaches to limit the role of faculty in the institution: they may limit the benefits accorded to full-time faculty, hire part-time faculty in lieu of full-time faculty, or both. Regardless of their approach, a trend toward more jobs at R institutions relative to jobs at P and PS institutions would be threatening to traditional notions of the academic profession.

Summary

In this chapter we have sought to integrate institutional strategies in the four key revenue markets by introducing the notion of financial health. Financial health at once determines and is determined by the interaction of resource allocation strategy and markets. Our statistical analyses suggest that the lessons from our twenty-six site visits are applicable to a broad range of institutions. The stories we have emphasized in the case studies are examples of phenomena that can be found in every segment of the U.S. higher education industry.

Private R institutions are tuition driven and therefore the most responsive to customer needs, especially demands by students for career-related education. Many public R institutions are also highly responsive to the career needs of students, especially if the state government is aligned with student demands. Financially healthy institutions can be found among all strategy types: P, PS, and R; broad and narrow scope; two-year colleges through research universities.

Many institutions seek to expand their degree offerings their scope and pursue a prestige-seeking resource allocation strategy. PS institutions run the risk of financial ill health because they face difficulty meeting the demands of present customers who generate the institution's revenue while, at the same time, making large investments in prestige-building activities. PS institutions may risk current reputation or prestige in one area for a mere chance that they will achieve prestige in a broader strategy. For private institutions with substantial endowments, a PS resource allocation strategy often means jeopardizing the endowment in order to pursue prestige. If the investments do not pay off, as is frequently the case, such an institution may be forced to retreat from prestige seeking in some or all areas. The institution will then be at a serious disadvantage compared to competitors that did not jeopardize their endowments to pursue prestige. Even PS institutions without an endowment are taking similar substantial risks.

Prestige is indeed rewarding in the U.S. higher education industry. The rewards of prestige include: more flexibility to select students and grant financial aid, lower teaching loads for faculty, higher private giving, and larger state appropriations. But the pursuit of prestige is a risky venture for institutions. It may also not be in society's best interest. We continue this theme in the concluding chapter.

Notes

1. One administrator suggested that accreditation agencies are a third customer of the institution.
2. Since our visit to University E, the institution has approved an academic planning document which appears to reaffirm the commitment to undergraduate education and commits the institution to "assess existing graduate programs. . . in terms of their contribution to the nexus of scholarship and undergraduate education."
3. This reflects the tendency toward homogeneity among P and PS institutions.
4. If institutions are subsidizing federal research activities with other funds, this implies that the federal government is able to leverage its own investment in basic research, getting more research value for every federal dollar spent. We return to this issue in the concluding chapter.
5. Private institutions often claim that the actual cost of providing an undergraduate education is much greater than the tuition charged. This would tend to discount the notion that tuition revenue is used to leverage federal research dollars. However, these statements about the cost of undergraduate education are difficult to evaluate—the measured costs likely include activities that support research rather than teaching. The issue of "cross-subsidy" is one deserving further attention.
6. At University B, one student indicated that he had chosen the university because he could sense that it was becoming more and more prestigious. This student recognized that there was less funding for current academic programs because the university was pursuing prestige, but he enrolled anyway. He said his bachelor's degree would become more valuable in the future as the university enhanced its prestige.
7. Group 1 corresponds to Carnegie Classification Baccalaureate II (less selective undergraduate colleges). Group 2 corresponds to Carnegie Classification Baccalaureate I (more selective undergraduate colleges). The companion volume provides further details on the calculations in Figures 5.7 and 5.8.
8. Our framework is not developed enough to firmly classify institutions according to our P/PS/R framework using available statistics. However, for certain classes of institutions, existing categorization schemes provide a rough approximation. As described in the text, it is common for public institutions tend to pursue prestige through research, and the Carnegie Classification scheme generally reflects different levels of research prestige as well as degree offerings. Group 1 with degrees through the master's level corresponds to Carnegie Classification Master's I. Group 2 with degrees through the doctoral level corresponds to Carnegie Classifications Doctoral I and II. Group 3 corresponds to Carnegie Classification Research Universities II (moderate federally sponsored research). Group 4 corresponds to Carnegie Classification Research Universities I (highest federally sponsored research).
9. The effect of unionization on faculty salaries has been studied extensively. See, for example, Rees, Kumar, and Fisher (1996).
10. We do not observe for-profit institutions pursuing PS strategies because shareholders are unlikely to be willing to bear the cost. These schools typically have faculty without tenure or with minimal attachment to the institution, reducing their ability to push for changes that increase their consumption and drive up costs. The next section discusses faculty power in these institutions.

6

Conclusions: The Implications of Prestige Seeking

A New Way of Thinking about Higher Education

In this book we have described the results of a two-year study of higher education in the United States. Adopting an "industry" perspective and drawing on case studies of twenty-six institutions around the country, we have focused on the conduct of higher education providers as they serve customers in the four key revenue markets of student enrollments, research funding, public fiscal support, and private giving. In examining the conduct of providers in the industry, we have focused on the nature of competition among schools and the strategies schools pursue. We identified, in Chapter 3, a series of important decisions that shape the character of each institution. First is the decision whether to pursue prestige through any or all of the three prestige generators: student quality, research funding, and sports. Institutions are also shaped by decisions about the level and breadth of their offerings in each of these three markets as well as other markets. Institutional decisions about how much to invest in reputation shape institutions as well. Our conclusion is that institutional variation in the industry is due in large part to the strategic choices made within each institution on these dimensions.

There is no single model of excellence in the higher education industry. Both reputation and prestige are positive assets for providers of higher education. Some institutions choose to invest in prestige, while others choose not to invest in prestige. Some institutions, especially those that are not pursing prestige, invest resources in their reputations for customer service.

133

Prestige seeking compels institutions to perform better than their competitors, thereby continuously raising industry standards for student admissions, research, and athletic competition. At the same time, the pursuit of prestige is expensive and risky. The industry as a whole does not appropriately balance the benefits and costs of prestige seeking because all stakeholders are not accorded equal voice in resource allocation decisions. Traditional institutions are governed largely by administrators or tenure-track faculty members, who reap the benefits of prestige if the institution is successful, but bear few of the costs. The costs, instead, are imposed on current students, adjunct or part-time faculty members, private donors, and state taxpayers. The costs of prestige seeking can place tremendous strain on an institution's financial health, leading to a financial "crisis." This sort of crisis is a product of institutions' ambitions for prestige, rather than external circumstances.

Prestige seeking is a strategic choice. While many schools are pursuing prestige, other institutions have opted out of this game and achieved success by identifying and efficiently meeting the needs of students. These dynamic institutions are transforming the landscape of U.S. higher education by adapting their educational programs and delivery methods to the needs of students. On the whole, this phenomenon appears beneficial, but one concern is that these institutions, especially for-profits, may ignore the objectives of the larger society in favor of narrow demands from current students.

Our examination of industry conduct led to the development of a classification scheme for institutions based on a combination of their investment strategy (are they investing in prestige and/or reputation) and their current stocks of prestige and reputation. Because of its primary importance to an understanding of the conduct of providers in the higher education industry, we often describe institutions with reference to their strategic type, that is, as prestigious (P), prestige-seeking (PS) or reputation-based (R). Our system also describes PS-R hybrids, which pursue prestige while investing heavily in reputation-based programs. This schema provides a new way of thinking about higher education—a different method of categorizing schools on the basis of their observed behavior. A college with a high level of prestige (i.e., a "P institution") exhibits characteristics that distinguish it from a school that does not have a high level. For example, reputation-based colleges and universities are typically dependent on students for revenue (or on state government funds related to

numbers of students) and gear their operations to meeting these customers' needs—they are outward looking. The most striking Rs are for-
profit institutions, which focus their activities in specialized and profitable markets. On the other hand, prestige-based schools typically have
multiple sources of revenue, which frequently include substantial private giving and federal research dollars.

The enhanced revenue-generating ability of P institutions stems
from one or more of what we term "prestige generators": the quality
of incoming students, the amount of federal research funding, and
sports programs. Having a more selective student body, receiving a
large amount of federal grants, and having a winning football or
basketball team allow a college or university to gain prestige, which
makes it easier to raise future revenues and provides protection from
environmental or policy changes such as demographic downturns
or cuts in state funding.

Prestige seeking has important implications for the performance
of the higher education industry. For example, it tends to promote
excellence as schools are continuously driven to improve specific
aspects of quality in order to improve their standing in the higher
education hierarchy. However, prestige seeking, which often requires
institutions to undertake investments in prestige in order to improve
standing relative to other schools, is a risky and costly path to follow. Developing and maintaining prestige through these generators
is expensive and necessitates a reduction in resources allocated to
other uses, especially for PS institutions. For example, the pursuit of
prestige through federal research funding can provide a strong incentive for an institution to reduce resources allocated to teaching
undergraduates. A sustainable and financially healthy position requires substantial and successful investment for an uncertain payoff. A PS strategy forces schools to meet enough external demands
to bring in revenue while making large investments in prestige-building activities, often resulting in declines in the quality of service for
the institution's current customers. Our site visits documented the
hard choices that PS institutions make when they find resources to
invest in prestige seeking.

Recent Interest in Prestige Generators

At the time we conducted this study, our perspectives contrasted
with much of the writing about higher education. That appears to be

changing, as five recent articles from the *Chronicle of Higher Education* show that appreciation of our prestige drivers is spreading. The first set of articles concerns sports, especially Division I-A football. We read in the *Chronicle* that a number of institutions are building these Division I-A football programs:

> Buffalo is hardly the first university to think that playing sports at an elite level would bring it fame and fortune. Ten other institutions have jumped to Division I-A [in football] in the past decade. (Lords 1999)

The core of our notion that sports success is a prestige driver is the sense that success in sports has a halo effect, spreading success to other institutional functions. This sense is aptly captured in another article:

> According to the conventional wisdom, a winning football team—much more than any other sport, even basketball—has immense payoffs for an entire university. Winning teams make alumni, fans, board members, donors, students, and prospective students happy, and so the university prospers when its team does. Donations go up, applications go up, and the money pours in from fans, bowl payouts, and television contracts. (Suggs 1999b)

Seeking prestige, we have pointed out, is a costly and uncertain endeavor. Colleges must divert investment capital away from other demands and focus on the prestige generators they are trying to build. As Suggs (1999a) puts it, "There is one certainty for administrators of big-time sports programs, however: If you want to compete at the highest level, it's going to cost you a lot of money."

As institutions focus on prestige investments, they allocate resources away from other activities, often to the consternation of faculty outside favored enterprises.

> Buffalo's woeful performance has led to heavy criticism from some faculty members and students, because the move to Division I-A—which cost the institution several million dollars a year over the last few years—comes at a time when the budgets of many academic departments are being cut. (Lords 1999)
>
> Marion (Buddy) Gray, a history professor and president of the Faculty Senate, says faculty members have been divided over whether the Wildcats' football success has overshadowed the university's academic endeavors. "I don't hear a lot of complaining, but there's a general sense of, 'We've had enough'" chest-thumping about football, he says. (Suggs 1999b)

In some cases, there is a payoff for all the expense. As we have said, the payoff is the halo effect that spreads success over many endeavors. Sometimes this is best described as an intangible: being a "real university."

Meanwhile, at Kansas State, the no longer mild 'Cats have given the university a national presence that cannot be achieved by any other means, according to professors and administrators.

"Kansas State is not Moo U.," says Mr. Herspring, the political-science professor. "Do people come here because of football? No, but they know who we are because of football. They at least know it's a real university." (Suggs 1999b)

The *Chronicle* has also carried articles about undergraduate students as a prestige driver. As we noted in Chapter 4, institutions that seek prestige can employ financial aid strategies to target students they might not otherwise be able to attract and thus improve prestige through enhanced undergraduate admissions. This strategic financial aid is also known as tuition discounting, since desirable students pay a discounted rate to attend the institution.

Bill Hall, a California-based financial-aid consultant ... noted that market forces have taken over—another way of saying that students now hold the upper hand. Colleges that refuse to offer discounts to students from middle- and high-income families, he said, will find themselves losing such students to other colleges. (Gose 2000)

Gordon Winston, an economist at Williams College, said it would only be a matter of time before the Ivy League institutions started offering merit scholarships—abandoning their pledges to award aid based solely on need. The Ivies, flush with huge endowments, will "force each other to a minimum possible price" in their zeal to enroll the top students, Mr. Winston said. Students' net costs may reach zero—or they may in fact be paid to enroll—much as prized graduate students today gravitate to programs that offer them the best compensation. (Gose 2000)

Like investments in sports, this strategy sometimes works, dramatically improving the prestige of an institution.

To be sure, some institutions have benefited from the freewheeling financial-aid environment of the 1990s—and officials at those institutions don't seem to have as much angst. Carnegie Mellon University has been able to sharply raise its national standing by steering more aid to high-achieving students, and by matching aid offers from other institutions—a practice that many colleges claim to avoid. Two-thirds of Carnegie Mellon's undergraduates come from outside Pennsylvania, up from just 17 percent a few decades ago. (Gose 2000)

Beside strategic use of financial aid, colleges have other tools to increase their share of talented undergraduates (and manipulate other key indices as well). One of the most rapidly growing phenomena in admissions is "early decision."

For colleges and universities, early decision offers a number of advantages. It represents a way to lock in a significant proportion of high-caliber students without having to worry about their being lured away by a competitor. It also enhances an institution's yield—the proportion of those admitted who enroll. That may seem like an arcane matter, but yield is a measure calculated in the *U.S. News & World Report*'s popular college rankings. Although its weight in determining the rankings is very small, some institutions look for even the tiniest of edges. (Sanoff 2000)

This recap of recent articles in the *Chronicle*, all of which appeared after we completed the first draft of this book, confirms that our description of prestige generators is right on track. We expect to hear people inside and outside higher education speak with increasing frequency in these terms in the years to come and hope that we have provided in this book a useful lens through which to interpret comments like the ones quoted here.

A Better Understanding

We have developed and applied a new framework to higher education in the United States. The framework seems useful in understanding the conduct of institutions in this industry and helping to shed some light on industry performance. But it is informed from a limited set of site visits. Furthermore, the site visit protocols did not contain this framework, so we could not ask respondents directly about some of the concepts that emerged as part of the framework. As a result, we do not explicitly know how our interview respondents themselves would view our taxonomy of institutional strategies. We did circulate a manuscript to all twenty-six institutional presidents and several of them wrote to us to express their admiration for the work we have done. Nevertheless, we could not systematically ask people like our interviewees how they view the concepts of prestige and reputation as affecting their institutional strategy. A future study based on surveys or an expanded program of visits would be able to answer questions like this.

Surveys based on our framework would allow us to make statements about a much broader set of institutions. These methods would help to confirm that we have appropriately described institutional strategies and allow researchers to classify many more institutions. One challenge is to write questions that respondents will be able to answer in a useful way, since we observed that many of our interviewees did not think directly in terms consistent with our framework. The template we used to document the collection of interviews at each campus (reproduced in the Appendix under the heading "Documentation of Site Visits") offers one way of structuring questions about strategy within each market, financial health, and overall resource allocation.

Quantitative research would be valuable as well. It is possible to develop a detailed set of specifications for which budget items or other numeric indicators describe or correlate with resource allocation strategy, degree mix, and scope. Zemsky, Shaman, and Iannozzi (1997) have started on this path for the student market. It would be interesting for these or other researchers to extend this numeric indicator set for our other markets and prestige generators.

We believe our framework has substantial utility outside the United States. The framework was developed to organize data from U.S. institutions, however, and may not apply exactly the same way in other countries. In particular, we conjecture that the prestige generators may differ in other countries, especially when viewed at a detailed level. In many countries, sports teams may confer no prestige on institutions of higher education, for example. In smaller countries, the types of research that confer prestige may be more limited or different from those in the United States. It is possible that some countries have no prestigious or prestige-seeking colleges, only reputation-based colleges that serve local needs. Site visits or surveys in countries outside the United States would yield valuable information about how prestige is attained in different societies and the distribution of prestigious, prestige-seeking, and reputation-based colleges and universities.

Getting to the Corner of the Position and Strategy Cube: Expanding Scope, Degree Level, and Prestige Seeking

Thinking of higher education in terms of an institution's strategic type rather than more traditional categorizations, such as sector of control, type of degree offered, faculty quality, or research funding provides useful insights into the dynamics of the sector and the implications of changes in the industry's operating environment. One of our clearest conclusions is that a large number of institutions pursue prestige and seek to expand their scope and increase the level of their degree offerings. We introduced the cube in Figure 6.1 as a shorthand summary of the many elements of position and strategy in an institution: whether to pursue prestige at all, through which of the prestige generators, and what level and breadth to operate with in each of the revenue markets. In theory, institutions could adopt a strategy at any point in this space that is consistent with their current stock of prestige; we observed such heterogeneity in the context of our site visits. Specifically, in our site visits we observed a prestigious, broad community college; a broad, reputation-based research institution; and a more narrow, prestigious research university.

In spite of this diversity, we perceived a strong force pulling institutions into the top left-hand corner of the cube—toward a prestige-seeking or prestige-based resource allocation strategy, increased scope, and higher degree level (offering more advanced degrees and research activities). We observed this movement in the direction of the arrows shown on Figure 6.1, despite the risks associated with such a strategic choice.

If one looks at all institutions of higher education over the past thirty years, it is apparent that there has been an increase in the number of institutions offering higher degrees. Some traditionally two-year schools began offering four-year degrees. Bachelor's-degree granting colleges and universities added master and doctoral pro-

Figure 6.1
Moving toward the Corner of the Position and Strategy
Cube or Remaining Stable

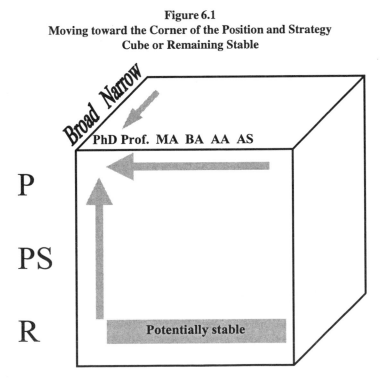

grams and schools once focused on undergraduate and professional education moved into research. Rarely have institutions reduced their degree level. Similarly, many universities have added programs and subject fields to their rosters over the past twenty years. Some aspects of prestige-seeking resource allocation strategies among institutions also appear to have increased (for example, increased competition for federal research dollars), although this may be limited by the overall stock of prestige available (which is discussed later in this chapter).[1]

Colleges and universities must work hard to balance this tendency to expand programs with the facts that it is easier to build and maintain prestige in more narrow areas and that it is expensive to engage in prestige building in the first place. University E is an example of an institution that sacrificed some prestige when it broadened its scope and degree offerings. Some of the most successful institutions, such as University A, are those that have maintained this balance, but even this is no simple matter. Shifts in market conditions can make a change in program focus necessary. However, it is often difficult for institutions to change focus without increasing scope— colleges and universities find it easy to open new program, but difficult to close old ones. For-profit institutions appear to have mastered the art of transformation. College C is constantly adjusting its degree offerings (both content and level) in response to changing market conditions. In general, as Figure 6.1 shows, R institutions have the greatest possibility for a stable strategic position. R institutions do face pressure to expand degree level and scope for many of the same reasons that institutions pursue prestige, as we discuss below. But for those institutions that moderate or resist such pressures, R institutions can remain in a stable point in our cube.

Internal Pressures to Pursue Prestige

On the surface at least, there appear to be strong pressures that lead institutions to invest in prestige in this industry. We suspect that this may be related to institutional governance, that is, the structure of power over resource allocation decisions. Our limited site visits did not probe deeply enough in some instances to determine whether strategic decision-making power stems from administrator or faculty control over institutions (although it stems from one or both of these two groups in each institution we saw). However, not all schools succumb to these pressures; institutions with similar stocks of prestige and similar opportunities for cultivating prestige often make different decisions as to whether to invest in prestige. For-profit institutions, more than any other type of institution, appear to shun prestige building. The nature of governance in these institutions provides important clues as to what influences the decision to pursue prestige. For-profit institutions have a much more direct link between administrator's rewards and the value to stakeholders than do other institutions. The administrators answer to shareholders or their proxy in the form of boards of directors. In for-profit institutions, faculty and other insiders have little if any influence over the strategic choices made by administrators. Because profit, and often growth, are their motives, administrators in for-profit institutions must identify and serve a reasonably lucrative set of customers. As a result, it is profitable customer desires that keep a for-profit within the R strategic type. In nonprofit institutions, administrators are not compelled so keenly to serve profitable customer desires. Indeed many institutions, both public and private, solicit private gifts explicitly to enable them to serve unprofitable customer desires. But that insulation from the profit motive also allows the insiders to choose a strategy without full regard for its impact on external stakeholders: customers, donors, and state governments.

Such differences in governance structure likely have important implications for the decision whether to pursue prestige because the cost, benefits, and risks of prestige building are different for faculty and administrators than they are for other stakeholders. Specifically, administrators and faculty bear little of the cost of prestige building, reap much of the benefit, and, most important, bear little risk in the process. Instead, the costs are borne by customers such as students or state governments. The observation that for-profit institutions do not invest in prestige suggests that prestige building is not a financially sound investment in an objective market sense. It also suggests that administrators and faculty in traditional institutions provide the impetus for the pursuit of prestige because they are able to reap the benefits without putting much at risk. If the governance structure does influence prestige-seeking behavior, we should observe systematic differences between the governance structure of P and PS institutions, on the one hand, and R institutions on the other.

The pursuit of prestige may be encouraged by other factors as well. For example, states often use appropriations formulas that reward prestigious institutions. Employers provide greater rewards to students with diplomas from colleges with more selective institutional bodies. Alumni and others demand high-profile sports programs and are willing to support some of the costs. There may even be a natural human tendency to seek prestige or status (Frank 1985). Since only one institution can rank number one in a given group, schools will sort themselves into increasingly smaller groups and compete for rank within the smaller groups.

New Competitive Pressures and the Stock of Prestige

Our description of the higher education industry is necessarily a snapshot of current strategies and often reflects recent transformations. For example, we have described institutions that have built prestige substantially in recent years and those that have lost prestige. This observation leads to the question of whether the stock of prestige available in the industry is constant (i.e., whether prestige seeking is a zero-sum game), or whether it is related in predictable ways to certain factors, such as the number of students served by the industry or the available amount of federal research funding. We can consider these issues by focusing on the three prestige generators we identified: student quality, federal research funding, and sports teams.

The stock of prestige available through student quality is not directly related to the number of students served by the industry. To the extent that the growth in the number of students served also reflects growth in the number of students with high test scores and high school grade point averages, an increase in the number of students served by the sector would increase the available stock of prestige. This would be the case if the student population was expanding because of underlying increases in the college-age population or because of increased access to higher education to a group excluded from higher education for reasons unrelated to test scores and grades, such as women or ethnic and religious minorities. On the other hand, if an increase in the number of students served was due to expanded access to students with relatively low test scores and grade point averages, then the stock of prestige would not increase.

Similarly, the stock of available prestige would increase with an increase in the total (inflation-adjusted) amount of federal research funding. Since World War II, federal research has expanded in real terms, making it possible for a larger number of institutions to receive some portion of this money and invest in research activities. For both student quality and research funding, therefore, the stock of prestige available may fluctuate according to largely exogenous factors. On the other hand, the stock of prestige available from winning sports teams would appear to be relatively constant, as the number of teams who can be conference or national champions is limited. However, the stock of prestige can grow if the popularity of alternative teams increases (such as women's sports, other men's sports besides basketball and football, and college athletes competing in the Olympic Games) or public interest (and consequently television revenues) permits an expansion of key games, as has been the case with the proliferation of bowl games in men's football.

Competition among P and PS schools is heavily influenced by these exogenous factors. In conducting our visits around the nation, we expected to see a great deal of diversity of form, structure, and direction among higher education institutions. While we did see some variation, we were also struck by the degree to which college and university administrators had many of the same concerns—rising costs of attracting students, increasing competition for federal research funding even as federal budgets expand, and increased state oversight. These are the concerns of schools wishing to pursue P and PS strategies in the context of external forces conspiring to decrease the amount of prestige available. Today federal research funding is growing in real terms, but will it grow fast enough to meet the investment ambitions of P and PS institutions? Although student populations are beginning to rise, it is far from clear where the resources will be found to fund the expansion of undergraduate education.

This environment is in sharp contrast to the post–World War II period. In that era, increased funding for research and broadened access to higher education among previously excluded groups implied that institutions could build their research capacity and the quality of their student body without harming those of other schools.

In the current environment, prestige seeking has taken on the qualities of a zero-sum game; when one institution gains, another loses. Most institutions reported that competition was increasing in most markets. For example, state governments have started lifting some of the traditional barriers to competition among public institutions and have demanded that they demonstrate the value of their activities in the belief that this will encourage them to meet the needs of their student and government customers better. Further, as higher education markets mature, existing schools look for new, "higher-margin" activities, yielding greater market segmentation and providing students with more options.

Regardless of whether the stock of prestige is growing or shrinking nationally, some aggregate shifts in the stock of prestige appear to be going on among different niches, among institutions in different states, and between sectors. For example, women's colleges became less attractive to many female students in recent decades as women gained access to traditional all-male colleges; most recently, however, they may be experiencing resurgence. The same may be true of historically black colleges and universities. Another national phenomenon is a geographical shift in the amount of prestige available, particularly to public institutions. It appears that schools in states that are increasing spending on higher education and where the population is growing have greater opportunities for prestige building, whereas schools in states that are restricting spending on higher education and are experiencing population declines have less access to prestige. In other words, we are witnessing a general shift in the amount of prestige from the *snowbelt* to the *sunbelt.* Although many Northern and Central states have a strong tradition of excellence in their public universities, we foresee increasing difficulty for those institutions that continue to depend on their state's appropriation to maintain prestige. Anticipating this trend, some of the most prestigious institutions have diversified their revenue mix, especially increasing the importance of research and private giving.

Finally, there seems to be a shift in the stock of prestige from private to public institutions. On the student side, this shift appears to be driven by tuition increases, which spur a self-reinforcing process of student migration from private to public institutions. As more high-quality students move into the public institutions, the prestige of the public institution increases and, along with it, the value of the degree relative to private institutions. This phenomenon was first witnessed in states like California and Michigan, but it appears to be spreading throughout the nation. Competition for the prestige generators leads to shifts in the stock of prestige across different types of institutions. There are also changes in the rewards of prestige, leading different types of institutions to invest in different prestige generators at different times. For example, in the last decade, many state governments grew less generous with funding for higher education. Some states have also started linking funding to specific performance measures. As a result, many public institutions have focused on private giving, generating increased competition between public and private institutions. Historically, private institutions were rewarded for prestige through private giving and public institutions, through the state government. However, overall trends indicate that for the past two decades state funding for higher education has been declining and that private giving has been increasing slightly.[2] In the mid and late 1990s, state funding increased strongly in many states. Nonetheless, we note that if the willingness of state governments to reward institutions for prestige declines, the net rewards of prestige may decline unless the industry comes up with ways of generating additional private giving. Similarly, the rewards of reputation are changing. While state governments are less likely to write "blank checks" to P and PS institutions than in the past, they appear willing to fund R institutions that can demonstrate that they are serving the public.

The *Pseudo-Crisis* in Higher Education

An important implication of these arguments regarding the stock of prestige and competition in the higher education industry is that *if* institutions continue to opt for a P or PS strategy in the current environment, it will appear as if the sector is in "crisis." If the stock of prestige is either stable or declining due to factors largely beyond the control of any institution, then investments in prestige seeking will become more risky. Institutions may continue to pursue this path despite some of the risks involved, in order to satisfy internal constituents. It is likely that some of these institutions will find their strategies to be inconsistent with long-run financial health given the new realities; these institutions will face a financial crisis. But it is this *choice* to undertake a particular resource allocation strategy that generates increased competitive pressures and leads to a picture of the sector in crisis. Hence, the term *pseudo-crisis* may be more appropriate. It is the aspirations of colleges and universities themselves that gives rise to many of the problems facing the industry—market opportunities may be becoming inconsistent with internal goals.

The Prestige-Seeking Dichotomy

We began our investigation with a series of apparently conflicting statements about the performance of the higher education industry and questioned how an industry that is world renowned for high-quality output could at the same time be disparaged at home as wasteful and in need of reform. When one looks at the U.S. higher education sector in a global context, one is struck by the widespread access and the preeminent research of America's colleges and universities, both of which are positive attributes. Higher education improves an individual's access to high-paying jobs and is positively related to health status and quality of life. The sector has produced technological, medical, and other breakthroughs in research, contributing to economic and social development. Yet the sector is also admonished in some quarters for escalating costs, lack of attention to student needs, and inefficiency. Our framework based on institutional strategies can help explain this apparent paradox of the sector: prestige seeking promotes excellence on the one hand but can lead to excessive expenditures and unresponsive schools that neglect the needs of some undergraduate students and other customers who don't contribute to institutional prestige.

Prestige seeking is a positive force in the industry in the sense that it encourages institutions to compete for high-quality students and for federal research funding. Competition for prestige pushes P and PS institutions to funnel resources into research and activities that help attract high-quality students. This benefits the federal government's research programs and the select group of students over whom the schools are competing. This competitive process generates the quality research and educational institutions that are the envy of the world. No institution, no matter how prestigious, can rest on its laurels because another institution is waiting in the wings, striving to attract research funding or students from that institution.

However, the excellence toward which institutions are striving may have little to do with the satisfaction of basic customer demands. For schools trying to build prestige, there can be a negative impact on students either because this strategy induces resources to be diverted from their basic instructional function or because the costs lead to tuition increases that exceed inflation. Institutional prestige increases the value of a degree in the labor market for students, and it may pay for some consumption benefits for students. But although students who are able to gain entry to prestigious institutions benefit, that benefit ultimately stems from the institution's ability to exclude some potential students from the institution. Students at PS institutions may get neither the value added that they could get from R institutions nor the signaling value of P institutions; these schools are presently sacrificing current consumption in order to build future prestige. Further, competition for prestige in the student market does not encourage institutions to improve the quality of educational delivery.[3]

Institutions compete aggressively for students via price discrimination—the strategic use of financial aid and merit scholarships—in order to increase the yield of students with the characteristics that contribute to prestige (high test scores, certain demographic characteristics). It is difficult to fund this aid, however, without hiking tuition for other students or using other sources such as endowment income. To deal with this problem, many institutions are beginning to adopt two-tiered admission programs, essentially lowering admission standards for students who can pay the full tuition but offering generous scholarships and "financial aid" to bright students often, regardless of their financial need. While this strategy may help an institution boost prestige in the short run, it does not appear to be viable for most institutions in the long run. If the difference between the quality of paying and nonpaying students grows too large, the quality of the market signal, and ultimately the prestige of the institution, will decline. The biggest losers in the process are the students who desire the signaling value of a degree from a prestigious institution but who are not wealthy and do not have the characteristics that contribute to prestige. Not only are these students less and less likely to be able to afford private P schools, but because of the increased price differential between the public and private institutions, they are less likely to be admitted to a prestigious public institution.

Prestige-seeking behavior in the research revenue market induces many institutions to expend resources to build and maintain research facilities. The fixed costs involved in building and maintaining a research infrastructure are large. The federal government is able to leverage its own expenditures on research with private and state money. This leveraging may benefit society by inducing private donors and state governments to support research activities, but it is not clear that this "cross-subsidization" is good for students. The results might also be an inefficient number of institutions investing in research infrastructure.[4] Many large private sector companies have reduced the size of, or even eliminated, their research laboratories and now rely on contracts with universities for research. This phenomenon suggests that universities have other customers who are absorbing many of the fixed costs involved in supporting the research infrastructure, thus allowing higher education to offer industry an attractive price for research services. However, financial pressures and decreased willingness on the part of state governments to subsidize research activities appear to be driving many universities to try to appropriate some of the economic rewards of research activities through technology licenses or equity stakes in high-tech spin-off firms. To the extent that universities succeed in capturing some of these technology benefits, the universities' gain is industry's loss.

The Evolution of the Higher Education Industry: The Dynamic Reputation-Based Fringe

The widespread prestige-seeking behavior of many colleges and universities creates an opportunity for other schools, pursuing an R strategy, to focus on the students that the PS institutions ignore. The conduct of R institutions has implications for the performance of the higher education industry. The high level of access promoted by the U.S. higher education industry is in large part the result of strategies pursued by R institutions and competition among them.[5] Revenue flowing into these schools is tied to student attendance; financial health is directly related to the ability to attract students. As a result, R institutions have a strong incentive to focus on meeting student demands by providing services that offer a large personal benefit to the student, especially in the form of consumption benefits (which for some students may be an enjoyable time, but for many is convenient class schedules), economic advancement, and knowledge. Because R institutions are competing with one another for student enrollments, they are driven continuously to improve the quality of the services they provide and to offer a variety of service bundles, thereby satisfying many different market niches.

The ability to bundle services in a way that reflects customer demands allows these institutions to draw new students into the industry. Many individuals, particularly those who are older than the traditional college-age student, are not interested in many of the extra-curricular activities and programs that are commonly associated with the "college experience" and do not want to pay for them. What they are willing to pay for is convenience: they don't care whether the school has a student union or an orienteering club but do want classes and administrative services to be offered at convenient times and locations. Many of the most dynamic, entrepreneurial institutions in the industry are tapping into this student market; often they are the for-profit schools. Public R schools do not face the same competitive pressures, since they often enjoy geographical monopolies on student enrollments and because public subsidy allows them to maintain low prices. However, even among publics, the level of competition is increasing, leading to greater attention on customer service as well.

These trends are generally positive ones for students because they imply that institutions are focusing on meeting customer demands. However, this goal often conflicts with the goals of the faculty, who are key constituents of the higher education industry but not customers. The customer focus of Rs leads them to treat faculty more like commodity labor, promoting specialization and the use of faculty time in activities that directly benefit the institution. Practically, this implies high teaching loads, monitored output, and less time for research. This is taken to an extreme in for-profit institutions, where faculty members do not receive tenure and serve solely as instructors, with no time for research and little role in course or program development. This trend is antithetical to traditional notions of the professorate and is frequently disparaged in the academic literature. This segment of the market has eliminated traditional notions of faculty members as stakeholders.

Although R institutions have a strong incentive to address the demands of students and provide services that generate a high level of private value added to the student, they do not have a strong incentive to meet societal objectives that no one is willing to pay for. The increased prominence of for-profit providers raises concerns that some societal objectives will be neglected. This is a potentially important failure of a competitive market for higher education. Students will generally not be willing to pay for educational services that do not provide them with some personal benefit. These types of services, if they can be identified, are ideal candidates for public subsidy. As the private benefits from higher education increase, it is worth asking whether state governments should continue to subsidize a wide range of educational activities or whether the public might be better served by their focusing funding in areas and toward needs that the private sector cannot or will not meet.

This book began with a puzzle related to the performance of the higher education industry: how can the U.S. higher education industry be maligned as wasteful and inefficient and at the same time be the envy of the rest of the world? We have argued that such a schizophrenic assessment of higher education stems from a tendency to assume that all colleges and universities are striving toward a single model of excellence, that of the prestigious research university. This study has explicitly recognized the diversity of the higher education industry by highlighting the strategic decisions that college and universities make, in particular, the decision to pursue prestige. Public attention has long been captured by the colleges and universities that have been successful in the pursuit of prestige. Yet, institutions that have shunned this strategy—which we call R institutions—are the ones transforming the nature of higher education at the end of the twentieth century and the beginning of the twenty-first.

Notes

1. A goal of future research is to determine if it is possible to develop a set of objective criteria based on an institution's characteristics and resource allocation data that may be used to classify an institution as following a P, PS, or R strategy. In this event it would be possible to observe whether or not in fact there has been an increase in the number of institutions pursuing P and PS strategies and their correlates.

2. This decline in state funding was reversed starting in 1997-1998, which saw a 6 percent increase. It is too soon to tell whether this represents a long-term reversal of the declining trend of the past two decades.

3. Some institutions (more P than PS) have developed niche markets that include significant attention to educational delivery and emphasize the rigor of their curriculum in marketing to prospective undergraduate students.

4. Prestige seeking also has an impact on the academic workforce. It increases competition for faculty who can generate research dollars. This implies that the best researchers in disciplines with substantial research funding benefit through higher salaries, institutional research support and lower teaching loads. Competition among institutions for these researchers creates a disparity between the faculty in "hot" well-funded fields and faculty members in other fields who do not receive such generous remuneration. This disparity is greatest at PSs investing resources in prestige; in such institutions there is often a great disparity between the teaching loads and salaries of faculty in departments that are targeted as potential generators of prestige for the institution and those of faculty in other departments.

5.   Whether such wide access to higher education is good for society is an open question. Critics have argued that increasingly college graduates are hired to perform tasks for which a high school diploma used to suffice, but it is very difficult to demonstrate in a convincing way whether public investments that encourage the pursuit of post-secondary schooling are or are not wasteful.

Appendix: Data Collection and Analysis

The case study visits formed the primary source of data for the analysis, supplemented by secondary source data described and cited in the main text. Following collection of the site visit data, the project team analyzed the reports to derive the strategy classification system described in the main text.

Sites Visited

Because confidentiality was needed to gain the cooperation and candor of the institutional representatives, we are not able to disclose publicly the names of the colleges and universities we visited. Instead, this appendix describes the way we selected institutions and summarizes their characteristics along a number of important dimensions.

We visited twenty-six institutions in four different states. The states were selected for geographical diversity and included one from each of the following regions: the South, Northeast, Midwest, and West. In addition, the states were facing different demographic and economic conditions.

In addition to variet of geographical region, individual institutions were selected in such a way as to reflect the variation of the higher education industry along several important dimensions, including type of control, scope of educational activities, and urbanicity. To summarize the scope of an institution's educational activities, we distinguished among institutions that have a research component, those that grant graduate degrees but do not engage in any amount of research, those that are primarily undergraduate institutions, and those that offer an associate degree. With respect to urbanicity, we distinguish among those institutions that are located in a major metropolitan area (urban), those located outside but in close proximity to a major metropolitan area (suburban), and those located in a small town or rural environment. Table A.1 reports the distribution of sites on each of these dimensions

Table A.1
Site Visit Characteristics

Characteristic	Number
Total Visits	26
Geographic Region	
South	6
Northeast	3
Midwest	4
West	13
Scope of Education	
Research	9
Graduate nonresearch	7
Primarily undergraduate	7
Associate's degree	3
Control	
Public	12
For-profit	2
Private nonprofit	7
Private religious	5
Urbanicity	
Urban	10
Suburban	13
Small town/rural	3
Resource Allocation Strategy	
P	6
PS	6
R	12
Hybrid	2

Data Collection Protocol

The one-day site visits were designed to help the researchers understand the market strategy and overall health of each institution as perceived by three different groups: administrators, faculty, and students. They were also structured to help us get a sense of the most salient issues facing the individual institutions and higher education in general. The teams generally consisted of two or three interviewers out of a total of six trained interviewers. The site visits were conducted between June and October 1996.

During a typical one-day visit, we conducted one-hour individual interviews with three administrators (the president, an administrator in charge of finances, and an administrator in charge of academics or admissions). We also conducted one faculty focus group and one or two student focus groups. In addition, we had time during the day to walk around the campus and observe things such as the state of repair of buildings, student interaction, and the presence or absence of communal spaces. The basic structure of the protocols is represented below.

Key questions asked on our visits included a section on the *individual's background*: What brought you to _____? How long have you been in this position? What was your position before you assumed this one?

We then focused on the individual's perceptions of *institutional mission, goals, and market niche*: What are the three most important goals for which this institution is striving? Is there a plan to help the institution achieve these goals? Is it a formal plan? Is it a strategic plan? Has it been disseminated? How did the institution arrive at this plan? How will you know whether or not you are achieving the goals? Do you have any system for evaluating progress toward the goals? What indicators do you use to evaluate the progress? What are the most significant challenges facing this institution today? How are you meeting these challenges? For whom are these challenges? Are you focusing on productivity improvement? Are you considering any major curricular reform? Are you contemplating structural change? Are you considering any changes in admission or aid policy? In what way has this institution changed over the past 10 years? What makes this institution unique? If you had to describe your institution in one sentence, how would you describe it? What is distinctive about your faculty? What is distinctive about instruction methods (curriculum)? What is distinctive about your outcomes?

What is distinctive about your research? What is distinctive about your philosophy/mission? What is distinctive about your student body? What other institutions do you tend to compare your institution with? What is the fundamental similarity between your institution and these? What distinguishes your institution from these? What is different about your (finances, social mission, student body, etc.) Do you systematically compare your institution with these? If so, in which areas?

We then asked about the *institution's constituents and the balance of power among them*: Which groups have the most important influence on the institution? In what ways is this influence manifest? Of the groups you mentioned, how would you characterize their goals (what they expect from the institution): students, faculty, staff, alumni, government, foundations, public, industry? Are the demands being placed on your institution by different groups in conflict? What are the most significant conflicts? How do you balance the demands in the event of conflict? Which constituents receive priority?

Subsequently, different respondents were asked a series of questions related to their area of expertise. We did ask most respondents about the *financial health of the institution*: Is the institution financially healthy? Why or why not? Have you made any significant changes in your operation recently in order to generate additional revenue? To curb expenditure?

Documentation of Site Visits

To encourage respondents to be candid, the interviews were not tape-recorded. Instead, interview teams took extensive notes. These notes were combined for each site and placed into a specially designed analysis template to highlight the market structure as perceived by each institution's respondents. As each set of interviews was placed into the template, the interviewers checked statements from the various interviews for consistency across interviews and with available documents or statistics from the institution. The template of that form is reproduced below:

Physical Description of Campus

Location: Describe setting of campus (urban, suburban, rural).
Relation to surrounding community: How is campus situated with respect to its community? Integrated or isolated?

Physical plant condition: What is the condition of the buildings? Are uses of buildings appropriate?

Campus Life

Student atmosphere: How many students are engaged in activities on campus, in public spaces? Major features of student life (fraternities, parties, intellectual climate).

Activity level: How much use does the space get? What types of uses?

Goals and Challenges

Goals and challenges: List and distinguish between goals and challenges (if possible).

Easily and well articulated? Consistent? Note how easily the goals and challenges were articulated and whether they were consistent among interviews.

How were they determined? Process and players.

Uniqueness: What makes this institution unique?

Realistic? Are goals and conceptions of uniqueness realistic?

Plans

Formal goals/mission statement: How are the goals documented?

Formal strategies: How are means and strategies documented?

Measurement and evaluation: What indicators are tracked and how are they compared?

Feedback: What influence does the indicator tracking have on allocation of resources or other behavior?

Student Markets

Descriptions: Which market segments?

Positioning: How does institution compare to others? On what dimensions? To which institutions?

Indicators of Market Position: What market signals does the institution use and how (e.g., rankings, accreditation, media, opinion)?

Awareness: How aware are leaders of the institution's market and position?

Health: How do leaders feel about the position in relative and absolute senses?

Strategies: What is the institution doing in response to the perception of its position and health?

Role of nontraditional providers: Are nontraditional providers competing in any market segments?

Faculty Markets

Descriptions: Which market segments?

Positioning: How does institution compare to others? On what dimensions? To which institutions?

Indicators of Market Position: What market signals does the institution use and how (e.g., rankings, accreditation, media, opinion)?

Awareness: How aware are leaders of the institution's market and position?

Health: How do leaders feel about the position in relative and absolute senses?

Strategies: What is the institution doing in response to the perception of its position and health?

Role of nontraditional providers: Are nontraditional providers competing in any market segments?

Revenue from Government Appropriations, Sponsored Research, Gifts, Grants, and Endowment

Descriptions: Which market segments?

Positioning: How does institution compare to others? On what dimensions? To which institutions?

Indicators of Market Position: What market signals does the institution use and how (e.g., rankings, accreditation, media, opinion)?

Awareness: How aware are leaders of the institution's market and position?

Health: How do leaders feel about the position in relative and absolute senses?

Strategies: What is the institution doing in response to the perception of its position and health?

Role of nontraditional providers: Are nontraditional providers competing in any market segments?

Costs

Descriptions: Which market segments?

Positioning: How does institution compare to others? On what dimensions? To which institutions?

Awareness: How aware are leaders of the institution's market and position?

Health: How do leaders feel about the position in relative and absolute senses?

Strategies: What is the institution doing in response to the perception of its position and health?

(Potential) Transformation

What changes? Describe any major changes the institution contemplated or will contemplate. Do changes involve markets or market segments? Production processes? Finance?

Mission change or change to support mission? Distinguish between changes that tend to support the existing mission and changes to new missions.

Actual or potential change: Are these changes in the past, present, or potential future? What would make change more likely?

Analysis

Based on the write-ups described above, the team first looked for general patterns in attempts to define useful categories for classifying strategies. Using a preliminary version of the schema described in the main text, each of the three authors separately classified the twenty-six site visit institutions along the dimensions of degree, scope, and resource allocation. The authors then met to resolve any ambiguities. The initial comparison indicated a high degree of agreement among the three authors. The few differences were resolved by defining the positions of the schema more precisely or recognizing that two institutions had substantial elements of two strategies (hybrid strategies).

We provided a draft of this book to representatives of all twenty-six site visit institutions for their review. We specifically asked representatives of the six institutions described at length in Chapter 5 to review their descriptions for any breaches of confidentiality or misrepresentations. In one case we made revisions to a description based on this review; those at the other institutions raised no objections to their portrayal. We believe this review enhances the credibility of the analysis we present.

References

Adams, Walter, ed. (1997). *The Structure of American Industry*. New York: Macmillan. Publishing Co.

Almanac of Higher Education (1995). Chicago: University of Chicago Press.

American Association of State Colleges and Universities. (1996). *Report of the States*. Washington: AASCU.

American Council on Education (1996). *Campus Trends*. Washington D.C.: American Council on Education.

Applebome, Peter. (1996). "Raising Standards Enhances Appeal of State Universities." *The New York Times*, January 10, A1.

Arenson, Karen. (1997). "Study Alters Criteria in Ranking Universities." *The New York Times*, March 19.

Astin, Alexander, William Korn, Kathryn Mahoney, and Linda Sax. (1995). *The American Freshman: National Norms for Fall 1995*. Los Angeles: Cooperative Institutional Research Program, American Council on Education and University of California.

Barron's College Guide. New York: Barron's.

Bishop, John. (1977). "The Effect of Public Policies on the Demand for Higher Education." *Journal of Human Resources*, 7(3):285–305.

Bottril, K. V., and V. M. H. Borden (1994). "Appendix: Examples from the Literature." In V. M. H. Borden and T. W. Banta, eds. *Using Performance Indicators to Guide Strategic Decision Making*. San Francisco: Jossey-Bass.

Bound, John, and George Johnson. (1992). "Changes in the Structure of Wages in the 1980s: An Evaluation of Alternative Explanations." *American Economic Review*, 82(3):371-92.

Bowen, H. R. (1981). "Observations on the Costs of Higher Education." *Quarterly Review of Economics and Business*, 21. 47–57.

Bowles, S., and H. Gintis. (1976). *Schooling in Capitalist America: Educational Reform and the Contradictions of Economic Life*. New York: Basic Books.

Boyer, Ernest L. (1994). *A Classification of Institutions of Higher Education: 1994 Edition*. Princeton, NJ: Carnegie Foundation for the Advancement of Teaching.

Brewer, Dominic J., Susan M. Gates, and Charles A. Goldman (2001). *In Pursuit of Prestige: Strategy and Competition in U.S. Higher Education, Technical Papers*. DRU-2541. Santa Monica, CA: RAND.

Brewer, Dominic J., and Ronald G. Ehrenberg (1996). "Does it Pay to Go to an Elite Private College: Evidence from the Senior High School Class of 1980." *Research in Labor Economics*, 15: 239–271.

Carmichael, H. Lorne. (1988). "Incentives in Academics: Why Is There Tenure?" *Journal of Political Economy*, 96: 453–472.

Carnegie Foundation for the Advancement of Teaching (1994). *Classification of Institutions of Higher Education*. Princeton, NJ: Carnegie Council on Policy Studies in Higher Education.

Carnegie Foundation for the Advancement of Teaching. (2000). *The Carnegie Classifica-*

tion of Institutions of Higher Education. Available at http://www.carnegiefoundation.org/ Classification/index.htm.

Chronicle of Higher Education. (1997). "An aggressive, For-Profit University Challenges Traditional Colleges Nationwide." June 6: A32–A33.

Clark, Burton. (1997). "Small Worlds, Different Worlds: The Uniqueness and Troubles of the American Academic Profession." *Daedelus,* 126 (4).

Clotfelter, Charles T. (1996). *Buying the Best: Cost Escalation in Elite Higher Education.* Princeton, NJ: Princeton University Press.

Computer Aided Science Policy Analysis and Research Database System (CASPAR), Version 4.7. Developed by Quantum Research Corporation for the U.S. National Science Foundation. Annual data system.

Cook, Phillip, and Robert Frank. (1993). "The Growing Concentration of Top Students at Elite Schools." In Charles T. Clotfelter and Michael Rothschild, *Studies of Supply and Demand in Higher Education.* Chicago: University of Chicago Press.

Cook, W. Bruce, and William F. Lasher. (1996). "Toward a Theory of Fund Raising in Higher Education." *The Review of Higher Education,* (20): 1: 33–51.

Corde, Colleen. (1997). "Congressional Earmarks for Colleges Increased by 49 percent for Fiscal 1997." *Chronicle of Higher Education,* (XLIII): 29, March 28.

Dibiaggio, John A., Steven B. Sample, and Gordon A. Haaland. (1996). "Confessions of a Public University Refugee." *Trusteeship* (May/June).

Dodd, Mike. (1997). "Winning One for the Admissions Office: At Colleges Nationwide, Athletic Victories are Boosting Academic Prowess." *USA Today,* July 11-13 (1997): 1A-2A.

Eide, Eric, Dominic J. Brewer, and Ronald G. Ehrenberg. "Does it Pay to Attend an Elite Private College? Evidence on the Effects of Undergraduate College Quality on Graduate School Attendance, *Economics of Education Review.*

Ellwood, John W., and Eric M. Patashnik. (1993). "In Praise of Pork." *Public Interest* 110:19–33.

Feller, Irwin. (1996). "The Determinants of Research Competitiveness Among Universities." In A. Teich (ed.), *Competitiveness in Academic Research.* Washington, DC: American Association for the Advancement of Science.

Fink, Micah, and Beth Saulnier. (1997). "Hard Choices: Universities Are Notoriously Slow to Change. But in the Nineties, Says President Rawlings, Cornell Must Be Quick, Lean and Agile." *Cornell Magazine* (May/June): 22–30.

Garvin, David. (1980). *The Economics of University Behavior.* New York: Academic.

General Accounting Office (1995a). *Student Loan Defaults: Department of Education Limitations in Sanctioning Problem Schools.* GAO/HEHS-95-99, June 19.

General Accounting Office. (1995b). *University Research: Effect of Indirect Cost Revisions and Options for Future Changes.* GAO/RCED-95-74, March 6.

General Accounting Office. (1996a). *Ensuring Quality Education from Proprietary Institutions.* GAO/T-HHEHS-96-158. Testimony given June 6, 1996..

General Accounting Office. (1996b). *Higher Education: Tuition Increasing Faster than Household Income and Public Colleges' Cost.* GAO/HEHS-96-154, August, p. 31.

Getz, Malcolm, and John Siegfried. (1991) "Costs and Productivity in American Colleges and Universities." In Charles T. Clotfelter, et. al., eds. *Economic Challenges in Higher Education.* Chicago: University of Chicago Press.

Goldberger, Marvin, Brendan Maher, and Pamela Ebert Flattau, eds. (1995). *Research Doctorate Programs in the United States: Continuity and Change.* Washington, DC: National Academy Press.

Golden, Tim. (1996). "Universities Find Foreign Donations Sometimes Carry Price." *New York Times,* December 9.

Gose, Ben. (2000). "Government Must Resolve Tuition-Discounting Predicament, Most Administrators Agree." *The Chronicle of Higher Education*, February 7.

Gose, Ben. (1999). "Web Site Lets Students Bid for a Degree." *The Chronicle of Higher Education*, October 1.

Grogger, Jeff, and Eric Eide. (1995). "Changes in College Skills and the Rise in the College Wage Premium." *Journal of Human Resources*, 30(2):280-310.

Gubernick, Lisa, and Ashlea Ebeling (1997). "I Got My Degree Through E-Mail." *Forbes*, June 16, 84–92.

Guernsey, Lisa, and Kim Strosnider. (1997). "Stanford Offers Plan for Alternative to U.S. News, Ranking of Colleges." *The Chronicle of Higher Education Daily News*, April 21.

Healy, Patrick (1997). "Penn State's Expansion Worries Competitors." *The Chronicle of Higher Education*, XLIII (29) (March 28).

Hopkins, David S. P. (1990). "The Higher Education Production Function." In Stephen Hoenack and Eileen Collins, *The Economics of American Universities*. Albany, NY: State University of New York Press.

Hopkins, David S. P., and William F. Massy. (1981). *Planning Models for Colleges and Universities*. Stanford, CA: Stanford University Press.

Immerwahr, John. (1997). "Enduring Values, Changing Concerns: What Californians Expect from Their Higher Education System." California Higher Education Policy Center, March.

Integrated Post-Secondary Education Data System (IPEDS). Washington, DC: U.S. Department of Education. Annual data system.

James, Estelle. (1990). "Decision Processes and Priorities in Higher Education." In Stephen Hoenack and Eileen Collins, *The Economics of American Universities*. Albany, NY: State University of New York Press.

James, Estelle, and Susan Rose-Ackerman. (1986). *The Nonprofit Enterprise in Market Economies*. New York: Harwood Academic.

Johnson, Kirk. (1996). "In Changed Landscape of Recruiting, Academic and Corporate Worlds Merge." *The New York Times*, December 4.

Kerr, Clark. (1997). "Speculations About the Increasingly Indeterminate Future of Higher Education in the United States." *The Review of Higher Education* 20(4):345–356.

Klein, Stephen P., Stephen J. Carroll, Jennifer Hawes-Dawson, Daniel McCaffrey, and Abby Robyn. (1995). "The Policy Implications of Interactions among Financial Aid Programs." *Journal of Student Financial Aid*, 25, (1) 5–11.

Kotch, Noah. (1997). "Yale, in Economic Ill-Health, to Put Resources Into its Top Programs." *The New York Times*, April 29.

Lee, Susan, and Daniel Roth. (1996). "Educonomics: Because What They Sell Is Such a Good Investment, Colleges Have Gotten Away With Obscene Price Increases. Not Much Longer." *Forbes*, November 18, 108–117.

Letts, Christine W., William Ryan, and Allen Grossman. (1997). "Virtuous Capital; What Foundations Can Learn from Venture Capitalists." *Harvard Business Review*, (March-April), 36–44.

Lords, Erik. (1999). "Move to the Big Time Yields Losses and Second Guessing." *The Chronicle of Higher Education*, (46), 16, December 10.

Manski, Charles F., and David A. Wise. (1983). *College Choice in America*. Cambridge: Harvard University Press.

Massy, William F. (1990). *Endowment: Perspectives, Policies, and Management*. Washington, DC: Association of Governing Boards of Universities and Colleges.

Massy, William F., and Charles A. Goldman. (1995). *The Production and Utilization of Science and Engineering Doctorates in the United States*. Stanford, CA: Stanford Institute for Higher Education Research.

Masten, Scott E. (1995). "Old School Ties: Financial Aid Coordination and the Governance of Higher Education," *Journal of Economic Behavior and Organization*, 28, (September): 23–47.

McKeown, Mary. (1996). "State Funding Formulas: Promise Fulfilled?" In Honeyman, Wattenbarger, and Westbrook, eds. *A Struggle to Survive: Funding Higher Education in the Next Century.* Thousand Oaks, CA: Corwin Press.

McPherson, Michael S. and Morton Owen Schapiro (1991). *Keeping College Affordable: Government and Equal Opportunity.* Washington, D.C.: Brookings Institution.

McPherson, Michael S., and Morton Owen Schapiro. (1993). *Paying the Piper: Productivity, Incentives, and Financing in U.S. Higher Education.* Ann Arbor: University of Michigan Press.

Morganthau, Tom, and Seema Nayyar. (1996a). "Playing the New Admissions Game: Colleges Accept More Kids Early, Leaving Fewer Spaces For Everyone Else." *Newsweek*, April 19, 58.

Morganthau, Tom, and Seema Nayyar. (1996b). "Those Scary College Costs." *Newsweek*, April 19, 52-56.

National Center for Education Statistics. (1995). *Digest of Education Statistics 1995.* Washington, DC: U.S. Department of Education, Office of Educational Research and Improvement.

Noll, Roger G., ed. (1988). *Challenges to Research Universities.* Washington, DC: Brookings Institution.

Office of Technology Assessment. (1991). *Federally Funded Research: Decisions for a Decade.* OTA-SET-490. Washington, DC: U.S. Government Printing Office.

Olivas, Michael. (1997). *The Law and Higher Education: Cases and Material on Colleges in Court.* Durham, NC: Carolina Academic Press.

Pascarella, Ernest T., and Patrick T. Terenzini (1991). *How College Affects Students: Findings and Insights From Twenty Years of Research.* San Francisco: Jossey-Bass.

Peterson's Guide to Four-year Colleges 1996. Princeton, NJ: Peterson's.

Peterson's Guide to Two-year Colleges 1996. Princeton, NJ: Peterson's.

Porter, Michael. (1980). *Competitive Strategy.* New York: Free Press.

Quigley, John, and Daniel Rubinfeld. (1993). "Public Choices in Public Higher Education." In Charles T. Clotfelter and Michael Rothschild. *Studies of Supply and Demand in Higher Education.* Chicago: University of Chicago Press.

Ray, Elaine. (1997). "Stanford Takes on U.S. News Rankings: Can a College Education Really Be Reduced to Numbers? Stanford Challenges the Newsweekly for Hitting a Little Below the Belt." *Stanford Today*, (May/June) 34–39.

Rees, Daniel I., Pradeep Kumar, and Dorothy W. Fisher. (1996). "Unionization and Faculty Salaries in Canada." *Industrial and Labor Relations Review.*

Ruppert, Sandra (1995). "Roots and Realities of State-Level Performance Indicator Systems." In G. Gaither, ed. *Assessing Performance in an Age of Accountability: Case Studies.* San Francisco: Jossey-Bass.

Ruppert, Sandra, ed. (1994). *Charting Higher Education Accountability: A Sourcebook on State-Level Performance Indicators.* Denver: Education Commission for the States.

Sanoff, Alvin P. (2000). "'Early Decision' Is a Gold Rush, With Many Left Out in the Cold." *The Chronicle of Higher Education*, January 21.

Scherer, F. M., and D. Ross. (1990). *Industrial Market Structure and Economic Performance.* Boston: Houghton Mifflin.

Schmidt, Peter. (1997). "Arkansas Study Questions Public Colleges' Use of State Funds." *The Chronicle of Higher Education,* XLIII, 22, February 7.

Selingo, Jeffrey (1999). "For-Profit Colleges Aim to Take a Share of State Financial-Aid

Funds. At a Time of Budget Surpluses, Lawmakers Are Extending Aid to a New Batch of Students." *The Chronicle of Higher Education*, September 24.

Sommer, John, ed. (1995). *The Academy in Crisis: The Political Economy of Higher Education*. Oakland, CA: The Independent Institute.

Spence, Michael. (1973). "Job Market Signaling," *Quarterly Journal of Economics*, 87:355–374.

Spring, Joel H. (1995). "In Service to the State: The Political Context of Higher Education in the United States." In John Sommer ed., The Academy of Crisis.

Stecklow, Steve. (1996). "Expensive Lesson: Colleges Manipulate Financial-Aid Offers, Shortchanging Many. Early Admittees and Others Are Eager, So Schools Figure They'll Pay More." *The Wall Street Journal*, April 1, A1.

Strosnider, Kim. (1997). "An Aggressive, For-Profit University Challenges Traditional Colleges Nationwide." *The Chronicle of Higher Education*, June 6.

Suggs, Welch. (1999a). "A Look at the Future Bottom Line of Big-Time Sports." *The Chronicle of Higher Education*, (46) 12, November 12.

Suggs, Welch. (1999b). "Wins, Losses, and Dollars." *The Chronicle of Higher Education*, (46) 12, November 12.

Toma, Eugenia Froedge. (1986). "State University Boards of Trustees: A Principal-Agent Perspective," *Public Choice*, (49) 155–63.

U.S. News & World Report (1996a). "1997 Best Colleges." September 16, 106–120.

U.S. News & World Report (1996b). "The Best Values: A Combination of Quality and Cost." September 23, 90–120.

Voluntary Support of Education. New York: Council for Aid to Education. Annual data system.

Wallace, Amy. (1997). "A Higher Name in Higher Education: Colleges are Recasting Themselves as Universities in Hopes of Luring Students, Faculty." *Los Angeles Times*, July 2, B2.

Weisbrod, Burton A. (1988). *The Nonprofit Economy*. Cambridge, MA: Harvard University Press.

Weisbrod, Burton A., and Nestor D. Dominguez. (1986). "Demand for Collective Goods in Private Nonprofit Markets: Can Fundraising Expenditures Help Overcome Free-Rider Behavior?" *Journal of Public Economics*, 30 (June): 83–95.

Weiss, Kenneth R. (1997a). "Community Colleges Recruiting Abroad." *Los Angeles Times*, September 15, 1997, p. A1.

Weiss, Kenneth R. (1997b). "More Colleges Filling Freshman Spots Early." *Los Angeles Times*, February 2, 1997, p. A1

Wildavsky, Aaron (1992). *The New Politics of the Budgetary Process*. New York: Harper Collins.

Winston, Gordon C. (1997). "Why Can't a College Be More Like a Firm?" *Change*, 29 (September/October): 32–38.

Zemsky, Robert, Susan Shaman, and Maria Iannozzi (1997). "In Search of Strategic Perspective: A Tool for Mapping the Market in Postsecondary Education" *Change*, 30 (November/December,): 23–38.

Index